CHROME

Brian Laban

CHROME

Glamour Cars of the Fifties

Photography by Laurie Caddell

GALLERY BOOKS
An Imprint of W. H. Smith Publishers Inc.
112 Madison Avenue
New York City 10016

All photographs in this book were taken by Laurie Caddell, with the exception of those in the introduction and of the Lincoln Premiere on pp 106–107, which were taken by Nicky Wright, the De Soto Adventurer on pp 64–67, photographed by Jonathan Barber, the Oldsmobile 88A on pp 16–19, by Bill Baker and the Buick Century Riviera on pp 112–115, photographed by Don O'Reilly.

We would like to thank the following owners who kindly made their cars available for photography:

Buick Century Riviera, Louis Matich, Casselberry, Florida *Buick Electra 225* Nancy Brewbaker, Anaheim, California *Buick Skylark* Ray Birkland, Anaheim, California *Cadillac Eldorado* Karl Riggins, Yorba Linda, California *Cadillac Eldorado Brougham* Ted Davidson and Herb Rothman, Yorba Linda, California *Chevrolet Bel Air Hardtop* Bob Wingate Classics Ltd, San Dimas, California *Chevrolet Corvette* George Primrose, Santa Maria, California *Chevrolet Impala* Clark Hansen, Sepulveda, California *Chrysler C-300* Ken and Diane Brody, Rowland Heights, California *Chrysler New Yorker* Bob Strenge, Phoenix, Arizona *Chrysler Town & Country Newport* Roy Luther, Anaheim, California *Continental Mark II* Samuella-Sue Kutger, Tulare, California *De Soto Adventurer* Arthur Brundage Jr, Oneonta, New York *Dodge Custom Royal* Dave Michalak, Milwaukee, Wisconsin *Dodge Custom Royal Lancer* Francis Becker's Auto Museum, Chandler, Arizona *Dodge Royal Convertible* Francis Becker's Auto Museum, Chandler, Arizona *Edsel Citation* Paul Cella, Monterey Park, California *Ford Custom Crestliner* Randy Carr, Fullerton, California *Ford Fairlane 500 Skyliner* George Richards, Canoga Park, California *Hudson Hornet* Dan Smilanick, Canoga Park, California *Imperial Crown* Dick Bales, Bell, California *Kaiser Hardtop Dragon* George Dunn, Long Beach, California *Lincoln Capri* Don and Gary Schwertley, Long Beach, California *Lincoln Continental Mark III* Dr Joseph P 'Jerry' Kutger, Tulare, California *Lincoln Premiere (red two-door)* Jeff Frank, Tustin, California *Lincoln Premiere (white two-door)* Bob Hodges, Yesterday's Wheels, Hartford City, Indiana *Mercury Turnpike Cruiser* Jeff Frank, Tustin, California *Oldsmobile 88A* Joseph Beck, Garden City, New York *Oldsmobile Super 88* Sam Donohue, Lansing, Michigan *Packard Caribbean* Stan Zimmerman, Beverly Hills, California *Plymouth Fury* Richard Carpenter, Downey, California *Pontiac Bonneville* Dr Milton Jacobs, West Bloomfield, Michigan *Pontiac 8 Convertible* Mrs J.F. Middlestetter, Encino, California *Studebaker Golden Hawk* Richard Gillies, Battle Creek, Michigan *Tucker* Peter Kesling, La Porte, Indiana

In addition to the owners of the cars featured in this book, we would like to offer special thanks to Ken and Diane Brody, Briggs Cunningham and the Briggs Cunningham Museum, Costa Mesa, California, Richard Dewey of the Ford Motor Company and Kurt Antonius of General Motors Corporation.

Published by Gallery Books
An imprint of W.H. Smith Publishers Inc.
112 Madison Avenue
New York, New York 10016

Reprinted 1988
1 2 3 4 5 6 7 8 9

ISBN 0-8317-1295-3

Contents

Printed in Singapore by Kim Hup Lee Printing Co Pte Ltd

Introduction

WORLD WAR II was over, America had celebrated victory and, rumblings in the Pacific notwithstanding, things were returning to normality; a spirit of optimism was abroad, and the prospect of unprecedented affluence was on the horizon. The American people had a reborn zest for life. Possessions were an expression of the good life; conspicuous consumerism (an old concept given a name at the turn of the century by American social scientist Thorstein Veblen) became a watchword, and nowhere was it pursued more fervently than in Detroit.

American cars of the 1950s were symbols of success – hugely different from the cars of the 1940s, and little wonder. The war stopped car production in the USA for most of the 1940s, and after 1941 car production stopped completely, in favour of arms production. After the war, shortages of cash and raw materials stifled any real novelty, and it was not until 1949 that the surviving manufacturers reverted with a vengeance to making a living from cars instead of from armaments.

Before 1949 most manufacturers simply facelifted tired pre-war models, within the constraints of money and materials, but the first cars of the 1950s brought a rush to be newest and best. The few remaining independents were quickest off the mark, mostly because they had less inertia than the big corporations and, thanks to war work, unaccustomed wealth. Sadly, this short-lived strength precipitated the downfall of many. New designs such as the revolutionary Tucker arrived just too early for the market's full recovery; as the Big Three held back their push into the 1950s, many independents were stuck with idiosyncratic cars which no one wanted but whose tooling costs dictated that they must live for five years or more. In the end it was George Walker's new Fords which set styling onto the new road.

Motoring glamour now took the nation's mind from continuing unrest and uncertainty. In February 1950 the US formally recognized the new state of Vietnam and began a military aid programme; Senator Joseph McCarthy made his celebrated charges against Communist infiltrators in the State Department, and the witchhunts began; in June, North Korea invaded South, and President Truman sent in the Navy and the Air Force – committing the US to a conflict which would drag on until July 1953. Meanwhile, Dwight D. Eisenhower had been elected President and cars were growing bigger, gaudier and more sophisticated.

In reality, most developments were about status – or what the advertisers sold as status. The size gap between the humble and the exalted was shrinking, through standardization, but identity remained all-important; mostly it came from styling. Everyone copied Cadillac's fins, and stylists like Harley Earl, Virgil Exner and Bill Mitchell became the industry's most important

people, but American popular cars were rediscovering engineering too.

Chasing sales, GM refined the automatic, Ford (via Lincoln) introduced ball-joint suspension and, eventually, everyone boasted overhead-valve V8s. As performance became another manifestation of status, power outputs soared, big engines went into small cars and even official disapproval of factory racing involvement failed to stem the performance tide.

Under the combined influence of ever more flamboyant styling and more horsepower per dollar, auto sales continued to rise, until the never-to-be-forgotten record sales year of 1955. Until then cars had adhered to the old standards, with heavyweight steel, real leather and cloth trim and barely a sign of plastic. In June 1955 the United Auto Workers union signed agreements with Ford and GM to protect pay during lay-offs, but in 1955 that was the least of the industry's worries, for they simply couldn't build cars quickly enough to satisfy sales demand and maintain quality.

It was not so much the fact that almost everyone had already bought a new car in 1955, but that far too many of those cars were demonstrating that they had been thrown together by rapidly falling apart again. While

the industry, gripped by the euphoria which only record sales can instil, planned for more, bigger and brasher, the market stood off. No matter that the 1956 Federal Highway Act authorized a long-term programme for the construction of 41,000 miles of new interstate highway for the forthcoming chrome cruisers, the buyers stayed away in their thousands. Eisenhower suffered his first heart attack, and depression loomed. Sales fell disastrously through 1957 and 1958 as the continuing slump in business activity pushed unemployment to almost 4.7 million. Stuck with huge and largely unwanted cars designed in the wake of 1955, the stylists fell to piling on the glitter in a desperate effort to liven up the market. The Edsel disaster was the most cruelly apparent example of what everyone was suffering: bad timing.

As the decade dragged to a close the country lost direction, and the cars somehow reflected it. The glamour was still there, and the power, but suddenly it was a more tawdry glamour. It was as though the automobile was marking time for another new start, and it certainly found one in the 1960s, with a youthful new President, regained confidence and some very different automobiles. The cars of the 1950s were unrepeatable.

Above: Briggs Cunningham and colleague John W. Burgess with the Chrysler-engined Cunningham C-5R Le Mans car of 1953. The horsepower race owed much to Chrysler and the hemi's development owed much to Cunningham's Le Mans exploits

Left: the 1948 Tucker had a rear-mounted, water-cooled, flat-six engine, derived from a Bell helicopter unit. It also had modified Cord automatic transmission, all-round independent suspension with rubber springing, disc brakes, a pop-out windshield and remarkable looks. Many of its advanced features were troublesome, and even unworkable, but in time the Tucker would have been right. Preston Tucker's postwar dream, however, was a victim of the courts. He was charged with fraud, on the dubious technicality that his few production cars differed from the plans initially shown to investors. Tucker was cleared, but the car was consigned to history

THE MAGNIFICENT 1950 Chrysler Town & Country Newport hardtop coupé is not a typical American car of the 1950s, nor even a typical American car of the 1940s, but more a spectacular and very beautiful anachronism, linking the 1950s with a bygone age of style. In that respect at least, the Town & Country Newport is typically early-1950s Chrysler. It took the corporation a little while to get into the swing of the 1950s, but it would have been a pity to miss such a glorious dinosaur as this.

Like the rest of Chrysler's contemporary seven-series line up, the Town & Country was very much engineering-oriented. Stylist Virgil Exner, soon to be Chrysler's saviour, had already joined the corporation, from Studebaker, but it would be a while yet before his influence was seen. Cars such as the Town & Country owed more to the 'build big' philosophy of the company President, K.T. Keller. Keller, who had succeeded Walter P. Chrysler himself, retired in 1950, but his ideas lingered a while longer.

The first Town & Country, with its distinctive, external wood framing, was one of the last introductions before America went to war in 1942. As a limited-production model it injected a little much-needed glamour into an otherwise dull range. 'Woodies', with their country club connotations, were by no means uncommon and, for a while, most manufacturers offered at least one variant. Most of them probably wished that they had beaten Chrysler to the perfectly evocative Town & Country name.

After the war the Town & Country reappeared in various guises, including one of the industry's first hardtops, a convertible and a variety of sedans. The series was gradually whittled down and the 1950 Newport was the last of the line. The Town & Country was, by any standards, a pretty huge car. It stood on an immensely strong, 131.5-inch wheelbase ladder chassis and it weighed well over two tons. While earlier Town & Country models had used genuine wooden construction, with mahogany veneer panelling on the ash frame, the later models were actually panelled with metal behind the timber, but at least Chrysler had the decency to paint the metal as metal, having rejected photographically simulated 'wood' trim. Others were not always quite so honest. The last Town & Country convertibles (the only models of 1949) were also the last genuinely wooden-bodied American convertibles.

The effect of the ash frame was undeniably elegant and Town & Country advertising was all about the hunting, shooting and fishing set. Sadly, that era was almost over. The wooden-framed bodies were beautifully fitted and solidly built but they also demanded a lot of care, such as regular revarnishing of the woodwork. In a culture increasingly dominated by

SPECIFICATION

Model 1950 Chrysler Town
& Country Newport

Engine type L-head str-8
Bore × stroke 3.25 × 4.875in
Capacity 323.5cu in
Compression ratio 7.25:1
Carburation 1 × 1bbl
Max. power 135hp
@ 3400rpm

Transmission Fluid Drive

Wheelbase 131.5in
Weight 4670lb

Price $4003

Preceding page: it may be a
hardtop, but the wood frame and
bulbous fenders mark the Town
& Country as a throwback to an
earlier era

Left: leather-trimmed luxury,
commanding an impressive view
of the road

Right, above and below: a name that
perfectly sums up the character
of the car. Other manufacturers
could only use the phrase in
advertising copy and wish they
had thought of it first

$4000, a substantial price tag in 1950.

Chrysler did offer some significant advances with the last of the Town & Country line, such as a padded safety dash, combined ignition lock and starter switch and 'Safety Rim' wheels to help a blown-out tyre stay on the rim. All these were carried over from the last of the convertibles. Nevertheless, the day of an automobile like this was really over. Bulbous separate fenders would have no place in the 1950s, as the 1949 Fords had rendered such features old hat. On the heels of 1950's slipping sales, 1951 marked the introduction of Chrysler's first V8, the legendary hemi, at the time of its announcement America's most powerful production engine. That was the key to Chrysler's future; the 700 or so Town & Country Newport hardtops sold in 1950 were an elegant reminder of its past. The advertising men were quite right to call them 'The Beautiful Chrysler'.

labour-saving gadgets and fast food, that was not a big selling point. Nor did wooden construction fit in with modern production demands. Real wood continued to be used on American cars for a few years more, mostly on station wagons, but it soon became another victim of tightening budgets and the change from craftsmanship to automation.

There were other changes, too, which the Town & Country had not yet caught up with. V8 engines, either flathead or the newly vaunted overhead valves, were becoming common but the Chrysler still relied on the big, lazy straight-eight, thumping out 135 horsepower from 323.5 cu in. Excellent though this engine undeniably was, it was rapidly becoming a throwback, much like the rest of the the car. With this engine and Fluid Drive the Town & Country was obviously far from being spritely, but it never pretended otherwise; nor, on the other hand, was it particularly cumbersome. Imposing would probably be the right word to sum up the big Chrysler. Driver and passengers sat more *on* the Town & Country than in it, perched high on superbly trimmed leather seats, to look down on lesser mortals. It was smooth, stately and more spacious than practically anything else on the road, and all for a little more than

THE CLAY STYLING model which would form the basis for the 1950 Ford Custom Crestliner was one of the first car designs for the new decade. It was also one of the last designs which the aging Henry Ford personally viewed and approved, before his death in April 1947. Henry saw George Walker's yellow-beige mock-up in 1946, pulled off a door handle, having mistaken it for the real thing, and said 'yes' to the basic shape. From the clay sprang the 1949 Ford and from the 1949 came the 1950 Custom Crestliner.

The model was crucial to the future of Ford. With old Henry gone, his grandson, Henry II, had taken the reins of the struggling company and was fighting back against losses running into tens of millions of dollars a month. Walker, a one-time semi-pro footballer and freelance industrial stylist, had only just been hired by Ford, as styling consultant. Later he would become a Ford Vice President, Director of Styling and 'father of the Thunderbird'. It is hard to believe that the series which he began for 1949 was, in effect, only the fourth major model change for Ford in almost half a century, following the Model T, Model A and the 1932 V8.

In June 1948 the 1949 models were introduced with a spectacular flourish, in the lavish setting of New York's Waldorf Astoria hotel ballroom. They were a huge and instant success, marking a new beginning for Ford. They also marked a new beginning for the styling ideas of others. The new shape was beautiful, different and deeply influential. Walker and his design team had replaced the typically bulbous moulded side and fender treatment of virtually every car of the day with a simple, integrated slab-sided look. Nowadays the 1950 Ford looks dumpy, but at the time those gently rounded lines, typical of Walker's previous industrial designs, gave the new Ford an illusion of having lower and lither lines than it actually had.

The 1950 Custom Crestliner carried the successful look a stage further, in a special-edition, two-door version. The basic design remained virtually unchanged for 1950 and, aside from the gleaming slab sides, the Ford was instantly recognizable thanks to its Studebaker-inspired 'spinner-nose' treatment, with its heavy chrome bar extending the full width of the grille-opening and wrapping round the front fenders, above the bumper. What mainly distinguished the Custom Crestliner externally was its striking use of colour. The company that originated the famous saying 'any colour you like so long as it's black' abandoned this dictum with the Crestliner, which had a very pleasing padded vinyl top treatment and a sweeping two-tone colour panel along its flanks, in the most vivid colours a customer could wish for. A survey in 1945 had shown that three out of four buyers wanted their auto in black, dark blue or grey, but the stylists believed otherwise.

George Walker, for one, believed in leading the customer towards new ideas. The limited edition was a good way of doing it, without forcing instant change.

The Custom Crestliner was different, with its better interior finish, flashy outside colours, whitewall tyres and rear fender skirts; Ford won the coveted Fashion Academy Award for styling in both 1949 and 1950. It was also vastly different from its predecessors in mechanical terms, and a huge step forward. The strong ladder chassis was Ford's first all-new offering since 1932; and the coil-spring front and long leaf-spring rear suspension, all with aircraft-type shock absorbers, were a far cry from the transverse leaf springs of old.

What Ford started with the Custom Crestliner was, in any case, what was going to happen to the car over the coming years – it quickly became the customizer's delight. Ford were happy to help: there were enough off-the-shelf options for the new Fords for every customer to drive away a personalized car loaded up to his heart's content – and, for the more radical, the Ford was ideal for sectioning, chopping and generally turning into something altogether individual.

Lesser Fords were available with a choice of a 95hp six

or the venerable flathead V8, but the Crestliner came only with the V8. In 1950 the motor was good for a round 100hp and, while it was not exactly red-hot, the 1950 Ford did have a slight performance edge over arch-rival Chevrolet. Where the bodywork was a joy to the customizer, the old flathead was something of a hot-rodder's dream, with plenty of cheap, off-the-shelf tuning potential as a legacy of its long standing. Having failed to buy in the excellent Studebaker auto as an option, Ford were still offering three-speed manual transmission, with or without overdrive (until the arrival of the none too special, two-speed Ford-O-Matic auto in 1951), and that was probably no bad thing.

The 1949 and, to a much lesser degree, 1950 Fords had something of a reputation for being loosely built and leaky, but their new clothes were enough to make up for that, and soaring sales marked the turning-point in the Ford fortunes. Sales for the 1950 model year were over a million cars, which was Ford's best result for twenty years, and although the Custom Crestliner sold only 17,601 examples in 1950 (and a total of 26,304 before it was discontinued in 1952) it had a lasting influence on the American car industry through the decade.

Pages 12–13 and far left: the clean lines of the new Ford led the way into the 1950s and led Ford out of deep financial trouble

Left: not all 1950s dashboards would be this simple

Below: Studebaker-inspired spinner nose – the first face of the 'fifties

SPECIFICATION

Model 1950 Ford Custom
    Crestliner

Engine type L-head V8
Bore × stroke 3.188 × 3.75in
Capacity 239.4cu in
Compression ratio 6.8:1
Carburation 1 × 2bbl
Max. power 100hp
    @ 3600rpm

Transmission manual + o/dr

Wheelbase 114in
Weight 3050lb

Price $1779

ACCORDING TO OLDSMOBILE's own advertising theme, the new Oldsmobile 88, with its good-looking 'Futuramic' styling, was notable for its effortless smoothness and its economy; according to anyone who drove one it was notable for the way in which it would make mincemeat of very nearly anything else on the road. Like it or not, and when they saw the sales figures they probably liked it, Oldsmobile with the 88 had started the era of real mass-market performance. Suddenly, the sort of 'go' usually only associated with the most exotic autos could be had in a low-priced family sedan.

Whether or not Oldsmobile felt they had to play down the performance image, the customers loved it and so, of course, did the racers; they leapt in where the ad men feared to tread and the secret was soon out – the 88 was a flier. In no time at all, Oldsmobiles became the cars to beat in the fledgling but immensely popular NASCAR late model stock car races. In 1949 the new Oldsmobile won six out of nine NASCAR races and 'Red' Byron became NASCAR champion with an 88. In May 1950 Hershell McGriff and Ray Elliot won their division in the first (and longest) Carrera Panamericana, or Mexican Road Race, their car 'City of Roses' beating assorted Lincolns, Cadillacs and foreign exotica in the process. In 1951 88s cleaned up almost half the NASCAR Grand Nationals, against growing opposition, and took the championship with some ease, from Plymouth, Hudson, Ford and Studebaker. Oldsmobile were no longer playing down performance, and the rest of Detroit was looking to catch up: the horsepower race was on.

It started with Oldsmobile's introduction of their first 'modern' overhead valve V8 engine, the Rocket V8. Designed by Gilbert Burrell with assistance from Pete Estes, the oversquare engine borrowed from the research into high compression engines done by Charles Kettering. It actually owed more to GM's overall research programmes than to the newly introduced Cadillac V8, which it was often accused of copying, and it was truly a milestone in engine design. It was light, smooth, flexible and incredibly strong, with a five-bearing crankshaft. In its original form it produced 135hp at 3600rpm and a very useful 263lb ft of torque from as low as 1800rpm. Had appropriate fuel octanes been available, the engine might eventually have run up to compression ratios as high as 12:1, but it started life at a relatively modest 7.25:1. Initially, the intention was to use this new engine only in the larger Futuramic series, the 98, but Olds General Manager Sherrod E. Skinner, overcoming the resistance of GM senior management, put the Rocket V8 into the smaller and lighter 76 body shell (in place of the standard straight-six) and called the car the 88.

'Make a date with a Rocket Eight' warbled the ads,

and the buyers did, in their thousands. By 1950 the Rocket 88 was outselling the other Oldsmobile ranges by two to one, and Tom McCahill called the car 'the best all-round highway performing production car made in America today'. With a manual gearbox it would turn 0–60mph in just over twelve seconds and even with Hydra-Matic the same sprint took less than a second and a half longer. Most testers reckoned it to be the first mass-production auto to top 90mph, and it handled and stopped too. All in all it was a winner.

It was improved somewhat for 1950, with a slightly stronger body on the unique-to-88 X-frame. In 1951 the 88 became the 88A, with few other changes, and a completely new line was added: the Super 88. The Super 88 joined the 88A and 98 as the three Olds series for the year, and it had an all-new body on a 120-inch wheelbase chassis – half an inch longer than the original 88 which had the same basic body as Chevrolet and Pontiac. Because of cost considerations, semi-elliptic springs were used at the rear, in place of the earlier car's coils, but if anything the Super 88 gave an even better ride than before. It was stable at high speed, with little body lean under hard cornering, and it was both responsive and forgiving, which was very useful to

buyers not yet used to this kind of performance. The engine was little changed since its introduction, although Oldsmobile had made sterling efforts to overcome problems of oil burning, overheating and valve burning. The Super 88 was little heavier than the original, so performance was still on the quick side.

Super 88s came in five body styles, distinguished by a one-piece windshield, a three-piece wraparound rear window and a number of trim differences from the 88As, but they were very much members of the same family. The best seller in the Super range was the four-door sedan, and the line-up also included the Holiday hardtop coupé, the Holiday having been introduced on the 88 as one of the very first hardtop models.

In spite of the continuing popularity of the sporty 88As and Supers, Oldsmobile sales slipped a little in 1951, partly as a result of shortages caused by the Korean war and partly because of the effects of tooling for the March introduction of the Super 88s. Race results were ever harder to come by too, as the new Hudson Hornet began to take up Oldsmobile's front-running role, but the 88As and Super 88s had done their job in establishing Oldsmobile's new image and setting the opposition a lead to follow.

SPECIFICATION

Model 1951 Oldsmobile 88A

Engine type ohv V8
Bore × stroke 3.75 × 3.438in
Capacity 303.7cu in
Compression ratio 7.5:1
Carburation 1 × 2bbl
Max. power 135hp
  @ 3600rpm

Transmission manual

Wheelbase 119.5in
Weight 3542lb

Price $2111

Preceding page: the beginning of the performance era

Facing page: 1951 interiors were relatively subdued – pinstripe upholstery and spartan instrumentation belied the character of Rocket 88 performance

Above and left: rockets were the way to go in the early 1950s and the 88A certainly did go

AT THE START of the 1950s Pontiac was regarded as one of the most conservative of the GM divisions, but the marque is really a remarkable success story. The name goes back to 1893, when the Pontiac Buggy Company took its name from its Michigan home town, itself named for the heroic Indian chief Pontiac of some 150 years earlier. In 1907 the Buggy Company began to build automobiles, but called them Oaklands; it was not until January 1926 that the first Pontiac appeared, as Oakland's cut-price stablemate. Within five years Oakland, a victim of Pontiac's success, was no more, and Pontiac went on to be the one and only marque ever created (as opposed to acquired) by GM which stayed the course.

When Pontiac's Silver Anniversary rolled around in 1951, Pontiac was a name to be reckoned with. They were in the industry's top five, with few mistakes behind them and what looked to be a promising future ahead. The Silver Anniversary range, introduced in November 1950, was a face-lift of the Harley Earl styled 1949 series – with some model rationalization. Earl's designs had been launched as the 'Smartest of All New Cars'. The stylish 1951 Pontiac was part of the noticeable transition from the pre-war to the post-war convertible, in a year when around one car in every thirty sold had a soft top and the 'modern' convertible really took off.

Pontiac had always been blessed with strong marque identity, and the 1951 Eight convertible was no exception. Like every Pontiac since 1935 it had the glittery hood appliqué, introduced by Bill Knudsen and known as the Silver Streak, and, like all Pontiacs, it was a lot of car for the money – $2388 in the case of the convertible. It sat on the same 120-inch wheelbase chassis as cars of the previous two years but it had lost the large teeth of the 1950 model from above the horizontal centre bar of the grille. Now it had just a pair of shining incisors flanking a V motif and an Indian head. Like the Indian head on the front of the hood and the Indian heads on countless previous Pontiacs, this one never smiled. The rest of the trim was simple and attractive. There was a chrome arrow along the sides, bearing the words Pontiac Eight, a chrome panel on the rear fender lower quarter and a chrome strip along the top edge of the cockpit, to suggest a dip of the body along the doorline. All in all, it was a very pretty and quite understated design.

Pontiac did not yet have a V8 engine, and the Eight of the name was a long-serving straight-eight which, since 1950, had grown up to 266.4cu in. V8s were obviously the vogue but the 116hp Pontiac was smooth, reliable and quite potent, if a trifle thirsty. Pontiac did not have a V8 until 1955 but, with the straight-eight's ample low speed torque, it nevertheless had a slight performance edge over the more powerful contemporary Chevrolet.

SPECIFICATION

Model 1951 Pontiac 8
   Convertible

Engine type L-head str-8
Bore × stroke 3.375 × 3.75in
Capacity 268.4cu in
Compression ratio 6.5:1
Carburation 1 × 2bbl
Max. power 116hp
   @ 3600rpm

Transmission Hydra-Matic

Wheelbase 120in
Weight 3568lb

Price $2388

Preceding page and above: good
looks, lots of trim and plenty of
equipment backed up the slogan
'Dollar for Dollar you can't beat a
Pontiac'

Left: the Silver Streak, one of the
most recognizable of all marque
identities

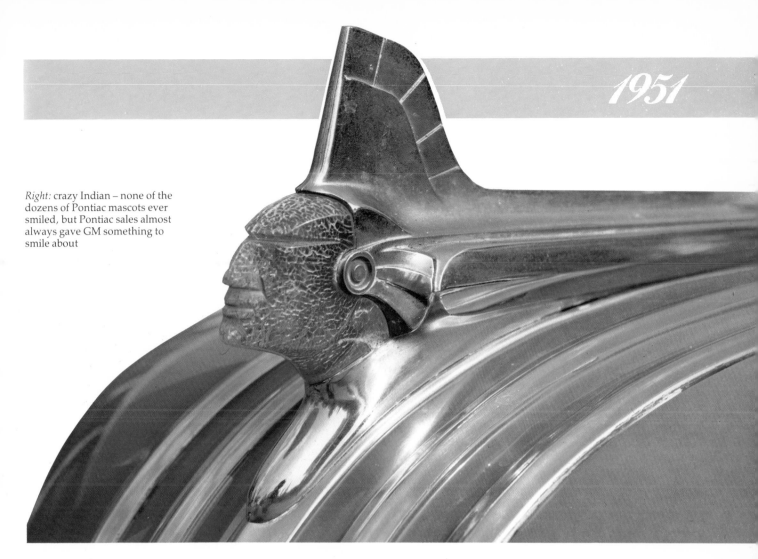

Right: crazy Indian – none of the dozens of Pontiac mascots ever smiled, but Pontiac sales almost always gave GM something to smile about

In fact, the Eight was considered to be fairly quick and it would run 0–60mph in under 14 seconds in manual trim, although not many owners bought manual Pontiacs – over eighty per centy chose cars with the optional Hydra-Matic transmission. The engine was set well forward in the chassis (which was a very rigid, cantilever, box-girder type) and the rear seat was set ahead of the rear axle and wheel cut-out, to give what Pontiac dubbed 'cradle ride'. Overall, the 1951 Pontiac was a little over 202 inches long, which was a touch shorter than the 1948 model but looked longer.

Looking bigger was part of the Pontiac secret of success. The marque had never really been a technological leader, or even a style leader, but it had always tried to offer a little bit extra and had generally succeeded. Pontiac's popularity was really about value for money and the division could genuinely advertise a lot more motor car for only a few dollars more. The 1951 Pontiacs offered more accessories than ever before, including such niceties as wheel covers, fender skirts, grille guards and sun visors.

The 1951 range, as ever, was another Pontiac winner, with total output approaching the division's best-ever figure and including the four-millionth Pontiac, built in August. Model year sales were over 370,000 cars and the Eight convertible actually outsold its six-cylinder sister. The attractive body style was continued until November 1952 with only minor cosmetic changes, but now with

the important additional option of dual-drive Hydra-Matic. The cars grew a little bigger for 1953, without much further change, but the completely modernized engine plant which would soon produce the new Pontiac V8 was already in business; it would be the starting point for a sporting new image for Pontiac which, by the end of the decade, would shake off its conservative tag to become king of the muscle-car builders. The old chief really should have raised a smile.

1953 WAS A special year for Buick – it was the marque's Golden Anniversary. It was also a very good year for Buick buyers. Buick had built a name for quality and performance and a reputation as style leaders. By virtue of having the all-new Riviera rolling off the production line by January 1949, this go-ahead division of General Motors laid claim to inventing the 'hardtop'. This low, steel top over pillarless side openings evoked the lean look of a convertible without actually imitating it. For the moment, Buick's rivals had only catalogue promises; the Riviera became a car to be seen in and, as the rest tried to catch up, Buick looked further ahead.

By 1953, and the Jubilee Year, Buick's engineering was all set to catch up with its styling. The year saw the introduction of Buick's first V8, an oversquare, overhead valve, 322cu in motor to replace the old straight-eight which had seen in more than one decade. The fine new engine was coupled to a new twin-turbine version of the maligned Dynaflow transmission. Twelve-volt electrics on the V8s and the option of power steering across the range were also introduced. Every car had been restyled at front and rear, with bigger grilles, new tail-lights, and headlights based on those of the XP-300 show car. And 1953 was also the year of the handsome, top-of-the-range Skylark.

The Skylark was a six-seater sports convertible, based on a 121.5-inch wheelbase Roadmaster chassis and derived from a home-brewed styling project by Buick's chief designer, Ned Nickles. Nickles was self-taught and a true extrovert. In 1952, inspired to a degree by European sports cars but perhaps more by Californian customizers, Nickles drew up plans to chop and change his own Roadmaster into something altogether more seductive. It was a purely personal expression and done on a strictly low budget, but the result was just the car that Buick needed to lead its 1953 line, and so Nickles' shoestring custom was translated into production.

In building the laudably practical Skylark, Buick resisted temptation to build a two-seater sports car and came up with a sister to Cadillac's new Eldorado and the Oldsmobile Fiesta, both limited production convertibles and each more expensive than the Buick's hefty $5000 price tag. In fact, the Cadillac, at $7750, was by far the most expensive car of the year. The 1953 Skylark was also a limited production model, and just 1690 were sold. More important than this modest sales figure, however, was the number of potential buyers of more mundane Buicks, enticed into the showrooms to ogle the supercar.

In terms of looks, the Skylark had a certain elegant simplicity. It was large but low, with a chopped-down windshield about the height of a letterbox and a sleek soft-top to match. It looked as good with the top up as it did with it down. Although like the rest of the 1953

range it did carry 'Sweepspear' side trims – also the brainchild of Nickles – it largely eschewed decoration. The Sweepspears were thin and extended over the sporty, full rear-wheel cutouts, accentuating the whitewall tyres and chromed Kelsey-Hayes wire wheels, which were the cheaper production alternative to the imported Borrani wheels of the prototype. Nickles' other trademark, the Ventiports, were missing.

The Skylark performed well too, at least in a straight line. The new V8, with four-barrel carb (pioneered by Buick in 1952), boasted an industry-leading 8.5:1 compression ratio and up to 188hp. It was 180lb lighter than the old in-line eight, and the Twin-Turbine Dynaflow was an altogether more lively proposition than the sluggish single-rotor original, though still nowhere near as good as GM's other auto, the Hydra-Matic. Nonetheless, it was sharper on take-off than its slushy predecessor and made for much-improved performance off the line, though still not in the hot-rod league. In fact, the Skylark was quite quick for its size; it could achieve 0–60mph in around twelve seconds, but there was no disguising the fact that, at over 17½ feet long, it was more at home on the turnpike than on the by-ways. The Skylark's suspension used coil springs all round and it rode on 8 × 15in tyres, large for the day but not for a car of the Skylark's weight. Power steering was standard, with the vagueness that that implied, but, that said, it handled well for the time.

The Skylark used the power-assisted brakes which were a Roadmaster option, and most of the time these would stop the 4315lb car quite effectively. Unfortunately the brakes were rushed into production with a faulty seal in the vacuum cylinder which, in some cases, let the fluid be sucked out of the master cylinder and into the engine. When the pedal was pushed a lot of smoke came from the exhaust but none at all was coaxed from the brakeless tyres. Buick, remarkably, left recall and repair to its dealers.

Inside, the occupants were cossetted in some style, with two-tone leather seats and a self-tuning radio with power antenna and even foot controls. There was also the luxury of powered windows and tinted glass, while the driver could gaze proudly at his own signature, sealed for ever in the centre of the steering wheel.

All in all, the 1953 Skylark was, and is, a most desirable automobile, handsome, sporty, generally well engineered and a worthy flagship for the revitalized range. In 1954 several of its features found their way to Riviera hardtops and convertibles, and would influence other models to come. With the emphasis on performance, 1954 Buick sales soared, but not, alas, on the strength of the restyled and downgraded Skylark which, in spite of a cut in price to $4483, sold less than 840 copies and led to the name being dropped for 1955.

SPECIFICATION

Model 1953 Buick Skylark

Engine type ohv V8
Bore × stroke 4.00 × 3.20in
Capacity 322cu in
Compression ratio 8.5:1
Carburation 1 × 4bbl
Max. power 188hp
  @ 4000rpm

Transmission Dynaflow

Wheelbase 121.5in
Weight 4315lb

Price $5000

Preceding page and left: the 1953 Skylark was simply beautiful, and the Sweepspear trademark was probably never used to better effect than on this milestone model. Chrome wire wheels, smooth sweeping lines and the lowest of rooflines are what give the big Buick its sporty and purposeful look

Inset: each Skylark steering-wheel centre bore a golden medallion inscribed with the original owner's name

Cadillac Eldorado

WHEN DWIGHT D. EISENHOWER was inaugurated thirty-fourth President of the USA, on 20 January 1953, he rode in the traditional motorcade down Pennsylvania Avenue in the back of a white Cadillac Eldorado convertible. No other car could have been more appropriate, for the new Cadillac was the undisputed cream of a classic crop in that milestone year for the American auto. In retrospect that first Eldorado has perhaps even grown in stature, and it remains one of the most desirable of all post-war American cars.

The very name Eldorado – from the legendary golden land of America's Spanish conquerors and, by extension and more to the point, any place where wealth is easily made – reflected the spirit of the day. These were the good times of post-war America, in spite of Korea and McCarthy, and nowhere was consumerism more con-spicuous than in the offerings of the auto industry.

Cadillac proclaimed its product 'the Standard of the World' and few cars could challenge that assertion. Since 1949 General Motors' annual shows had attracted hundreds of thousands of visitors, and the dream cars which were its centre-pieces told GM management just how much innovation the buying public would take. In 1953, when the shows gained the name Motorama, the corporation launched three sporty convertibles based on successful show cars of previous years, the Oldsmobile Fiesta, the Buick Skylark and the Eldorado. They were not simply badge-engineered sisters, but three distinct cars; and the Cadillac was their crowning glory. It was an automotive tour de force; there was no question of the Cadillac being a mere challenger to the likes of the esoteric Packard Caribbean: it stood alone.

The styling of the 1953 Eldorado simply exuded that brand of superiority which has no hint of brashness – that was for another market-place altogether. The Eldorado was a limited production, five-seat, two-door convertible in the super-luxury class. Behind Cadillac's first, massive example of a one-piece Dagmar bumper and grille swept flowing lines and a nipped waist, along with the industry's first wrap-around windshield and the inevitable Cadillac tailfins. Like other Cadillac convertibles, the low soft-top had a tiny, formal rear window and the obligatory chromed wire wheels. The power-operated top retracted between the rear seats and the trunk lid, where it was concealed beneath a clever, automatic metal tonneau which fitted flushly into the bodywork. This top, like the rest of the car, was beautifully engineered and it worked smoothly, quietly

SPECIFICATION

Model 1953 Cadillac
   Eldorado

Engine type ohv V8
Bore × stroke 3.812 ×
   3.625in
Capacity 331cu in
Compression ratio 8.25:1
Carburation 1 × 4bbl
Max. power 210hp
   @ 4150rpm

Transmission Hydra-Matic

Wheelbase 126in
Weight 4800lb

Price $7750

Above and following pages: 'the undisputed cream of a classic crop in that milestone year for the American auto'. From any angle, the 1953 Eldorado is a stunning motor car – by any standard

and reliably, every time. Inside, the car was superbly appointed, with two-tone leather upholstery (in a limited choice of colours to complement the paint colour), a padded dashboard, substantial sound-proofing under the hood and within the soft-top, and even a heated driver's seat. Some of the cars were fitted with air conditioning for warmer climates, and these rare examples are distinguished by air intakes above the rear fenders.

This was the era of the high-performance Cadillac and, although the division emphasized the Eldorado's smoothness and efficiency rather than actual horsepower, the latest Cadillac V8 was a real powerhouse. From the beginning, in 1949, this short-stroke, overhead-valve, 331cu in engine had been an industry leader. For 1953, with four-barrel carb, improved breathing and dual exhausts, it was good for a hefty 210hp, which was 30hp more than the early Chrysler hemi and five more than the Mexican-Road-Race-winning Lincoln. The extra horsepower enabled Cadillac to improve economy, thanks to a higher axle ratio, while retaining the sparkling performance. The Eldorado could achieve 0–60mph in just over 12 seconds, and on the other hand could better 18mpg on the highway. Although the Eldorado was intended to be equipped with the excellent Hydra-Matic auto, a fire at the Hydra-Matic plant cut off supplies for several months and some cars were adapted to use the stodgier Buick Dynaflow. Around one in six 1953 Cadillacs were fitted with Dynaflow.

To be sure, the Eldorado was never intended to be a sports car – a sporting car certainly but a sports car, no – as it was simply too big and comfortable. Yet it *was* capable of making quite rapid progress on most types of road, perhaps as a result of its engineering standards more than its suspension design, which was of the straightforward coil-spring and damper variety. As it had power everything else, the Eldorado naturally had power brakes, and there were few other cars to touch any Cadillac in terms of performance – not for a few more years at least.

The Eldorado was listed at a staggering $7750, which made it easily the most expensive car of the year. At that price it attracted 532 buyers, seventy-four more than the Olds Fiesta (which was some $2000 cheaper), but only around one third of the sales of the Skylark, in an overall convertible market of some 155,000 cars. It was all too good to last: the 1954 Eldorado was restyled, softened up and given more power as a palliative to more weight. It was treated to a huge price cut, down to $4738, and 2150 were sold. Then and now, the fortunate 532 who had bought the original Eldorados were the lucky ones. Theirs was the true classic, the definitive 'fifties convertible Cadillac.

IN DECEMBER 1947 NASCAR, the National Association for Stock Car Auto Racing, was formed by racing driver/enthusiast Bill France, and a group of friends, because the American Automobile Association would not sanction his idea for a championship stock car race. Within a few years NASCAR events for 'late model' sedans were to be virtually synonymous with stock car racing, and in the southern states the sport was to become even more popular than baseball or football. What attracted crowds then, and still attracts them now, is the fact that the cars driven by the Good Ole Boys, on the dirt and asphalt ovals, bore at least a passing resemblance to cars in the showroom.

NASCAR-style racing, which the AAA continued to promote in the north, called for a car with the right combination of power, handling and reliability. These desirable features had to come more or less as standard because, in theory at least, only very limited modifications were allowed. In the early 1950s there was really only one way to succeed in stock car racing, and that was to run a Hudson Hornet.

Hudson may not have been in the same league as any division of Ford, GM or Chrysler. the Big Three, in terms of sales or styling, but when it came to racing the Hornet was in a class of its own. Since 'stock' then meant something much closer to the truth than it does now, it indicated how good a car the Hudson really was.

The Hornet had had the same high beltline, sweptback, 'Stepdown' styling since 1948, for the usual reason of no money to make changes. What's more, it was also

stuck with what, on paper, was an outdated, outclassed, flathead six. In terms of sales, this stale combination was rapidly turning into an embarrassment. Even in the mid-price sector in which the Hornet was supposed to sell, buyers who did not want a racer were put off by a straight six and old-fashioned styling, when V8s and new looks every year were the norm. Any chance of a face-lift for the Hornet disappeared in 1953, when Hudson ploughed around $12 million, which it could ill afford, into a small and dowdy car to be called the Jet. Conservative engineering, shoestring finance, dated styling and weak selling kept Hudson sales to a trickle and brought losses running at around $1.5 million a month by late 1953, but on the circuits the Hudson bowed to none.

SPECIFICATION

Model 1953 Hudson Hornet

Engine type L-head str-6
Bore × stroke 3.812 × 4.5in
Capacity 308.2cu in
Compression ratio 7.2:1
Carburation 1 × 2bbl
Max. power 145hp
@ 3800rpm

Transmission manual + o/dr

Wheelbase 124in
Weight 3570lb

Price $2769

Above: from the side, the 1953 Hornet was certainly distinctive, but on the race track most rivals only saw a rear view

Following pages: Twin H-Power engine option was the first step towards racing success, but the Hornet was also a well-equipped and handsomely trimmed road car

The year 1953 saw the Big Three enter stock car racing, prompted directly by the success of the upstart Hudson. Hudson should have gone under in the build-up of big money factory involvement, which entailed some very liberal interpretations of the rules regarding factory optional equipment. Of course, Hudson offered options, but everyone else went to extremes – anything that did not carry a factory part number was simply labelled 'approved equipment'. In spite of this blatant rule bending, the Hornet was still a good enough car to carry the day.

The standard Hornet's 308cu in long-stroke six gave 145hp at a leisurely 3800rpm, and plenty of torque, already enough to give the 3570lb car quite lively performance. The optional Twin H-Power, twin carburettor, dual manifold set-up probably gave an extra 10hp, for even more 'go'. The very special, 7-X, 'police' engine, designated for 'severe usage' in 1953 offered Twin H-Power plus bigger bores, bigger valves, special high-compression cylinder head, a special camshaft and around 210hp. Marshall Teague, most famous of the Hudson tuners and winner of twelve out of thirteen 1952 stock car races, reckoned to be able to coax 112mph from a Hornet certified as 'stock' under NASCAR rules.

In 1953, with Hornets largely unchanged since their introduction in 1951, Frank Mundy won the AAA stock car championship and Herb Thomas won the NASCAR championship, against the might of Ford, GM and Chrysler. Hudson Hornets won twenty-two of the thirty-seven NASCAR Grand National races and thirteen of the sixteen AAA races.

The secret was in both the enthusiastic factory support and in the way the Hornet handled. It was a big, soundly engineered car, of unit construction with coil-spring suspension all round and it was both grippy and precise, with less body roll than most and far better

reliability. In sheer weight of numbers, too, Hudson had the edge, and three out of four Hornets to start a race would usually still be around when the flag fell.

Alas, the flag was soon to come down on all Hudsons. They kept winning stock car races with the virtually unchanged Hornet all through 1954, including the most prestigious Southern 500, at Darlington, and around half the other races they contested, but at the end of the year Lee Petty's Chrysler emerged as Grand National Champion. This was Hudson's swansong; the growing opposition had finally broken a run of championships going back to 1950. In May 1954 Hudson became the junior partner in the new American Motors Corporation and Hudsons gradually (though not immediately) became less Hudson and more Nash. In 1957, Hudson ceased production, as AMC capitalized on the success of the Rambler nameplate. Being a winner was not enough.

KAISER WAS NOT a good name for a car launched in 1946, even if its eponymous founder was a national hero; its teutonic ring might have evoked memories a little too recent for comfort. This problem was minor, however, when compared with the fact that, even with a new offering as good as the Kaiser undoubtedly was, the American public showed quite a remarkable resistance to any automobile that didn't emanate from Ford, Chrysler or GM. If only they had known what they were missing: every Kaiser was a little special for one reason or another, be it styling, practicality or just plain individuality; and the most special Kaiser of all was the 1953 Hardtop Dragon. Sadly, even it was incapable of bringing Kaiser the success it deserved and once looked set to achieve.

The company opened shop in 1945, when millionaire shipbuilder Henry J. Kaiser joined forces with Joseph A. Frazer of the Graham Car Company and took over the massive Willow Run plant in Michigan, where Ford had mass-produced B-24 bombers. At the time, Henry J. was widely regarded as the natural successor to Henry Ford as the American industrial hero, and he had massive government aid for his bid to break the Big Three stranglehold.

The prototype Kaisers of 1946 had front-wheel drive and all-independent, torsion-bar suspension, but the first production cars were sadly conventional and rather mediocre. They nevertheless sold like hot cakes and by 1949 Kaiser, with five per cent of the market, was able to raise $44 million from the Reconstruction Finance Corporation to fund its new model programme. The basic shape which would see Kaiser through to the end, and include the Dragon, was designed by Howard 'Dutch' Darrin and introduced in March 1950 as a 1951 model. It was sleek and beautiful and, for a while, Kaiser sales soared, putting the company into twelfth place in the sales league.

The car that Darrin designed was known as the Anatomic Kaiser and it was quite different from anything else on the market. It had a very low, rakish

SPECIFICATION

Model 1953 Kaiser Hardtop
Dragon

Engine type L-head str-6
Bore × stroke 3.312 ×
4.375in
Capacity 226.2cu in
Compression ratio 7.3:1
Carburation 1 × 2bbl
Max. power 118hp
@ 3650rpm

Transmission Hydra-Matic

Wheelbase 118.5in
Weight 3435lb

Price $3924

Preceding pages, left and below right: one of the tragedies of the 1950s was that being good was not always enough. Like most Kaisers, the gold-bedecked, Bambu-trimmed Dragon was a fine car, but it could not stop the company's ultimate downfall; even the man often dubbed 'the natural successor to Henry Ford' could not overcome the American public's extraordinary conservatism and, after his failure, few others would even try

look, with a beltline lower than any other at the time of its introduction, and which stayed lower than any other until after its demise. It also had an enormous amount of glass above the low waistline, far more than any rival, even the Lincoln Capri which ran a poor second. It came in two ranges initially, Special and Deluxe, and as a sedan, coupé, or Traveler, which was a very practical cross between a sedan and a station wagon.

In 1952 Virginian was added to the model names and Manhattan and Carolina soon followed, the Carolina being a stripped, cut-price model, allegedly intended to draw prospective buyers into the showrooms. Very few were sold. The Dragon, which was introduced in 1953, was exactly the opposite of the Carolina in every respect except a similar inability to attract customers.

All Kaisers were well known for the availability of bright colour schemes and interesting interiors, the latter from designer Carleton Spencer. Spencer designed a Dragon trim package in 1951 and it was on this that the 1953 Dragon was based. The body style was actually standard Kaiser; the Dragon retained the central pillars of the sedan and was a hardtop in name only, but the trim was unique and quite beautiful. The top, sweeping forward to the distinctive peaked windshield line, was finished in a padded vinyl material called 'Bambu'. This material was also liberally used inside the car, on a padded dash, on the door panels and inset into the attractively patterned cloth seats, while the floor and trunk floor were covered with good-quality carpet.

The padded dash was just part of a real effort on Kaiser's part to promote safety features in the car. The windshield popped out if struck hard from inside, and the instruments were recessed, years ahead of legislation. The Dragon was also a surprisingly agile performer, built with a separate and very rigid body on a light and low-slung chassis. In spite of the huge amount of glass in the top it had a low centre of gravity and excellent ride and roadholding.

Perhaps the biggest drawback in trying to sell the Dragon as an up-market car was the fact that it still had Kaiser's old straight-six engine, when others were offering more and more powerful V8s. Gold-plated badges, name-plates and hood ornaments, and even a gold plaque bearing the owner's name on the dash, were obviously no substitute for more cylinders and more horsepower. It didn't matter that the Dragon's torquey, 118 horsepower, 226cu in six was adequate and economical, nor that Hydra-Matic transmission, whitewall tyres and tinted glass were standard fittings; it still didn't have a V8 and it still didn't come from Ford, Chrysler or GM. Kaiser sales were on the way down, and in its single model year the Dragon sold only 1277 copies, often at well below the $3924 list price (slightly more than a Cadillac 62).

After the death of the Dragon, the range was revamped and a supercharger was offered as an option to bring the Manhattan up to 140hp. A fibreglass-bodied sports car, the Kaiser-Darrin, was offered, and Kaiser-Frazer merged with Willys, but none of this was enough. Dies and tooling were transferred to an Argentine operation and Kaisers of a sort continued to be made well into the 1960s, but Henry's dream really died with the Dragon.

PURELY ON THE basis of numbers sold, convertibles did not make a great deal of economic sense to most manufacturers, and it was this fact as much as the growing safety lobby which eventually led to their demise in the late 1970s. In the 1950s, though, convertibles were a glamorous necessity, dream cars of the showroom and boulevard which, by powers of brand-name association, helped to sell their humbler, tin-topped brethren to the masses. They were the ad man's dream, symbols of youth, style and flair; and like it or not, every manufacturer had to have one. For 1954, Dodge had two: the Royal and the Royal 500, one up-market, the other very up-market.

The Royal convertibles were handsome, well-built cars, typical of the new breed of Dodge, which reflected the marque's recent change of direction. At the beginning of the decade, Dodge, like most of Chrysler's products, had had a stodgy, down-beat image with dull, conventional styling and uninspiring six-cylinder engines. The traditional Dodge customer was typically the solid, respectable business type taking the next step up the social ladder from Plymouth. Dodge sold many cars, but sales were slipping.

Super-stylist Virgil Exner had joined Chrysler from Studebaker in 1949, and set out to revitalize the creaky image. The 1953 Dodge range was among Exner's first full-scale restylings for Chrysler, and the style carried over to the 1954 models with very few detail changes. The Coronet had been the top series in 1953, but for 1954 it was demoted to second place by the introduction of a new range, the luxurious Royals. The Royal convertible was among them, to do what convertibles were there to do: add the sparkle.

The new styling was a great improvement on the old and obviously played a major part in improving the Dodge image, but there was another and possibly even more significant change in 1953: the arrival of the Red Ram V8 engine as an across-the-range option. That the need for a V8 existed among the relatively up-market Dodge clientele was shown by the fact that more than sixty per cent of them specified it in its first year as an option. For the 1954 series, V8 power was standard. The Red Ram V8 was a fine engine, cousin to the Chrysler hemi introduced in 1951, and scaled down from 331cu inches to 241.3. It had a bore and stroke of 3.44 × 3.25 inches and a relatively low compression ratio, varying from 7.1 to 7.5:1, depending on the model. The ability to run low compression ratios, and hence make the most of low octane gas, was a result of the excellent thermal efficiency of the hemispherical combustion chambers which gave the engine its name. These chambers also allowed central location of the spark plug for better fuel ignition, and the use of large, well-spaced valves, with smooth porting. The 241cu inch Ram Jet engine

produced up to 150hp as used in the 1954 Royal and, as would become apparent, was capable of producing considerably more. It was also strong, economical and reliable. The drawback was that the engine was very expensive to produce.

With this engine, the light, compact car (smaller, lighter *and* more powerful than previous models) was a very lively performer. Dodges of 1953 took almost 200 stock cars records at Bonneville, and another Dodge recorded over 102mph on a dry lake in California. A very stiff, double-channel section chassis, coil-spring front suspension and non-parallel leaf springs at the rear also gave the 1954 Dodge splendid ride and handling. It was a natural for racing, and picked up many NASCAR wins at the expense of the aging Hudson Hornet and various GM products. In 1954, while the 'Road Race' Lincolns were dominating the big stock class of the Carrera Panamericana, Dodge V8s quietly scooped the first four places in the mid-size stock class. This reflected the changing emphasis at Dodge. It seemed that the division was no longer interested in the sort of customer it had once relied on: performance was now the message.

While it was not actually a race car, it was racing that created the very special Royal convertible of 1954, a limited-edition model known as the Royal 500 which commemorated the fact that a specially equipped Royal convertible had been chosen as the year's Indianapolis Pace Car. As well as the usual fine appointments of the Royal, the 500 series also had Kelsey-Hayes chromed wire wheels, a 'continental' spare wheel mounting, the top-of-the-range 150hp Red Ram engine, and special insignia. It sold for $2632, and 701 of the total of 1799 Royal convertibles for 1954 were 500 models.

Chrysler emphasized the comfort aspect of the new cars more than their performance, with advertisements such as 'You have never driven so much car so restfully ... so easily. These shining lengths of steel are beautifully tractable, wonderfully responsive and obedient to the lightest touch of your foot, your hands ... Discover the delightful floating-on-air sensation of these great cars in motion ...', but from here on Dodge was going to be all about speed and power, and Exner's stylish new designs. Dodge may have turned its back on its old customers, but there was a whole new market just around the corner.

Model 1954 Dodge Royal
    Convertible

Engine type ohv V8
Bore × stroke 3.44 × 3.25in
Capacity 241.3cu in
Compression ratio 7.5:1
Carburation 1 × 2bbl
Max. power 150hp
    @ 4400rpm

Transmission PowerFlite

Wheelbase 114in
Weight 3355lb

Price $2632

Preceding page: leader of the pack at Indianapolis, 1954, the Royal convertible followed an illustrious line of Pace Cars at the 'Brickyard'

Far left: 'continental' mounting for the spare wire wheel

Left and below left: Dodge were not slow to commemorate the convertible's leading role at Indy

THE 1954 LINCOLN CAPRI Custom Coupé was a real Jekyll and Hyde of a motor car. To all intents and purposes, it was simply another well-engineered, luxuriously equipped, not particularly fetching, early 1950s Lincoln. To an *aficionado*, however, the Capri is the 'Road Race' Lincoln – winner of the stock car division in three successive runnings of the gruelling Carrera Panamericana – and a highly prized collector's car.

The Capri was introduced in 1952, all-new and top of the rather unexciting Lincoln line-up. It and the rest of the Lincoln range remained on offer virtually unchanged for the next three seasons – the division was not strong on market-place impact at the time. Between 1952 and 1954, however, Lincoln enjoyed remarkable success and in the last of those years climbed to fourteenth place in the market with their best sales year since the war. Still, had it not been for its racing exploits the Capri might have been remembered as just another Lincoln.

The Capri was launched with a new overhead valve V8 to replace the 337cu in flathead, which had hitherto been used in everything from Lincolns to Ford trucks and which was an early hot-rodders' favourite. The new car had other advantages too, which soon had it pressed into service for racing, as Ford returned to motor sport for the first time since the mid–1930s.

In the year of their introduction, Capris took the first five places in the International Standard class (stock cars by another name) of the second (official) Mexican Road Race. The class-winning Capri, driven by Chuck Stevenson, finished the near-2000-mile race in twenty-one and a quarter hours, just over two hours behind Grand Prix driver Karl Kling's works Mercedes. Stevenson led the Lincolns to a 1-2-3-4 finish in 1953, when the race overall was won by the inimitable Juan Manuel Fangio in a Lancia (the European teams took this race, with its American market implications, very seriously).

The fourth and final official year of the Panamericana came in 1954 and, on paper, it saw the poorest result for the Capris, but as this still meant finishing first and second in class, it was not a cause for dismay. Moreover, the 1954 Capri was the definitive 'Road Race' Lincoln, similar in appearance but a great improvement on the already excellent original. The biggest difference was under the hood, where the 'showroom stock' power had risen over the previous two years from 160 to 205 horsepower. The 317cu in, overhead-valve V8 was a superb engine, made for tuning. It was very strong, with a rigid, deep-sided crankcase, and very smooth, owing to a crankshaft with eight counterbalance weights rather than the usual six. In 1953 it was the most efficient engine of the day. Even in standard form it was far better than the much-vaunted Chrysler Hemi and just ahead of the expensive Cadillac, although it lost out to the latter as most powerful engine of the year by just 5hp. It was also very torquey, offering 205lb ft at a low 2300rpm.

The wizards who tuned the 1954 winning car, which was privately entered and sponsored, were Bill Stroppe and Clay Smith, of Long Beach. With the help of factory-available options such as mechanical (rather than hydraulic) cam followers, 'truck' cams and oversize inlet valves, it was possible, within the regulations, to wring almost 300hp from the Capri.

No amount of power will help in road racing if the chassis is bad, but the Capri's chassis was extremely good. It was relatively compact, sitting on a 123-inch wheelbase, and very stiff, thanks to luxury car engineering. It was also blessed with excellent roadholding and brakes. At the front, the Capri pioneered ball-joint suspension, on MacPherson struts, which was much more flexible than the traditional king-pin system but perhaps not shown off to best advantage by the vague, recirculatory-ball power steering. At least the king-sized drum brakes were good, and factory options such as special front hubs and axles, 'export' suspension and non-standard final drive ratios were available. An otherwise standard Capri with a high ratio axle would reach a very impressive 130mph, and on the standard car, as equipped for the road, that included

carrying around a full range of power equipment, including four-way power seats, beautifully fitted leather and fabric trim and substantial soundproofing. In spite of the relatively short wheelbase, the Capri was very roomy and it had more glass area than any contemporary except the Kaiser. It also had the option of air conditioning which changed to fresh air ventilation when the pump was switched off.

The standard car weighed 4245lb and cost $3869; in racing trim it was stripped of most of the creature comforts and probably cost nearer $10,000, but it was a winner. Ray Crawford and Enrique Iglesias were the driver and co-driver who gave the Capri its final victory on the Carrera Panamericana. The 1908-mile route ran from Tuxtla-Gutierrez to Juarez, on roads varying from bad to worse and running from sea level to a height of 10,500 feet. The race was actually won by yet another Grand Prix driver in a European racing car – Umberto

Maglioli in a Ferrari. Maglioli averaged 106mph and Crawford took almost exactly three hours longer to cover the punishing course, at a remarkable average speed of over 93mph. That particular Crawford Capri retired with honour to Harrah's motor museum in Nevada, while Capris which have led the more sheltered half of the Jekyll and Hyde life can still be found cruising the countryside, ready to embarrass much more modern roadburners at the drop of a flag.

Preceding pages and left: the Capri's simple and unassuming lines belied the excellent performance of the three-time class winner of the Mexican Road Race

Above: 'the most efficient engine of its day', just made for tuning

SPECIFICATION

Model 1954 Lincoln Capri

Engine type ohv V8
Bore × stroke 3.8 × 3.5in
Capacity 317cu in
Compression ratio 8.0:1
Carburation 1 × 4bbl
Max. power 205hp
    @ 4200rpm

Transmission Hydra-Matic

Wheelbase 123in
Weight 4245lb

Price $3869

IN 1954 NASCAR, THE National Association for Stock Car Auto Racing, ruled that to be eligible for its hugely popular events, stock cars would have to be truly stock, rather than stock plus options as had been the case in the recent past. By 1954, having been shamed by the extraordinary run of competition successes from upstart Hudson, the Big Three were deeply committed to trying to attain NASCAR victories. The simple 1954 NASCAR ruling meant that the most powerful car that a manufacturer could race would be the most powerful car that they could advertise as a ready-to-roll, stock model; and the horsepower race suddenly took on a new and urgent meaning. Any manufacturer who had the slightest hope of competing in NASCAR – and most did – hereafter had to catalogue a whole car for the job, rather than listing speed equipment to add on to whatever basic model one chose. Chrysler wasted only two days after the start of the 1955 NASCAR season before unveiling, on 8 February, their trump card, the 300hp Chrysler C-300. It must have been something of a shock to others with pretensions to the NASCAR throne.

The 1955 C-300 was the brainchild of Chrysler division's then chief engineer, R.M. Rodger, but credit for its development must also go in large measure to Briggs Cunningham, who made enormous contributions to Chrysler engine design with his early-1950s Le Mans exploits, and to Carl Kiekhaefer, the controversial mastermind behind Chrysler's racing efforts, who subsequently turned the C-300 into one of the most formidable racing stock cars of all time.

The hemi-head V8, introduced in 1951, was the very heart of the C-300. Initially it produced a very modest 180hp but it was immediately obvious that there was much more to come. It was Rodger, with an eye on Cunningham, who realized that the hemi could realistically be persuaded to offer 300hp in stock form, with twin four-barrel carbs, 8.5:1 compression ratio and special cams. In 1955 he put the 300hp engine into a slightly modified New Yorker two-door hardtop shell, and this became the C-300. It did not take the advertiser's epithet 'The Beautiful Brute' to tell anyone who knew anything at all about autos that this was very special indeed: 300hp in a stock sedan was unheard of at the time. The C-300 was soon to begin to demolish the opposition on the tracks, but it was also quite docile and refined enough to be an exceptionally fast road car.

In fact, the C-300, and, indeed, most of the subsequent 'letter-car' series of Chrysler 300s, was a limited edition, less through lack of demand than for the fact that it required a fair amount of specialized work in its construction. The New Yorker shell was given an Imperial grille, and the standard suspension was substantially reworked to match the available horsepower, with special springs and heavy-duty shock

SPECIFICATION

Model 1955 Chrysler C-300

Engine type ohv V8
Bore × stroke 3.812 ×
    3.625in
Capacity 331cu in
Compression ratio 8.5:1
Carburation 2 × 4bbl
Max. power 300hp
    @ 5200rpm

Transmission PowerFlite

Wheelbase 126in
Weight 4110lb

Price $4109

Preceding page and far right: cars like the 1955 Chrysler C-300 were a direct result of the popularity of NASCAR-type 'stock' racing, with its demand for the use of a whole road-going package. Chrysler found the formula was also a winner for the road, and a long series of 300 'letter-cars' followed. Today, 'The Beautiful Brute' is as beautiful as ever – and still an exceptional performer

Right and inset, right: instrumentation on the C-300 was strictly functional, and included the rarity of a clock on the steering-wheel centre

absorbers. These were necessary adjuncts to the already good New Yorker package; the C-300 was not only fast but also big and luxuriously equipped, with such niceties as wire wheels and superb leather upholstery. Its wheelbase was 126in, its overall length was just short of 219in, it was over 6½ feet wide and it weighed almost exactly two tons. All this added up to a very dependable car and an exceptionally good handler.

The C-300 shot to prominence on its first time in competition, at the prestigious 1955 Daytona Speed Weeks. Kiekhaefer entered a single car, driven by Tim Flock, and that car recorded a two-way mile average of over 130mph, while other C-300s were only a couple of miles an hour slower. In the Grand National race Flock and another C-300 driven by Lee Petty were awarded first and second places after the winner on the road, Fireball Roberts' 1955 Buick, was disqualified for a technical infringement. Kiekhaefer Chryslers went on to monopolize the 1955 NASCAR results; at one stage they took sixteen consecutive wins in a remarkable demonstration of superiority, which left Flock champion with twenty-nine Grand National victories.

For once, Chrysler were not shy about advertising racing success and there was never much pretence that the C-300 was anything other than an outright performance car, but in many ways it was much more than this. It was a totally civilized and, in spite of its performance, very safe road car; and its racing exploits served mainly to improve the package still further.

Chrysler had got it exactly right when they combined the two symbols of power and quality in the C-300, and it showed the way that the corporation would be going for many years to come. In 1956 the hemi was strengthened to 354cu in and 340hp and the 300B was born, starting the run of annual model changes through the alphabet which earned the 300 series the name 'letter-cars'. It would run right through to the 300L, which appeared in 1965, and would include cars churning out as much as 390hp, but the first C-300 was one of the finest of the breed and, as the one that started it all for Chrysler and its rivals alike, it deserves to be remembered.

IT IS SOMEHOW difficult to think of Packard in terms of the 1950s: the hallowed name more readily evokes the 1920s and 1930s and a line of great twelve-cylinder luxury cars of incomparable style. The company did struggle on, however, until the late 1950s, and it did leave behind a classic Parthian shot, the Caribbean.

Until World War II the Packard had been a symbol of prestige, opulence and engineering excellence. In the post-war years the image was allowed to slip, as America's only surviving independent builder of luxury cars made the unforgivable social blunder of trying to sell a cheaper Packard. Those who could afford a real Packard felt demeaned and those who could not felt that the very name was somehow above their station. It was a fatal mistake, but before the great name was finally laid to rest the magnificent Caribbeans gave one last reminder of what Packard had once stood for.

The Caribbean convertible was introduced on 21 November 1952 for model year 1953. Packard was in the doldrums, only partly because of its misguided policy of undercutting Cadillac and Lincoln. The rest of the problem was that Packard could not afford much by way of post-war innovation, and its cars were dull. The engineering was still among the most respected in the industry, but 'Packard' no longer symbolized the pinnacle. By 1952 its plants were only working at half capacity to satisfy about three per cent of the luxury market, and there was a spirit of resignation about the company. In May 1952 James J. Nance took over the ailing organization from the elderly Hugh Ferry, and immediately decreed that the cheaper Clipper become a separate marque and that Packard's rightful role as a builder of quality cars be restored. He wasted no time in reintroducing big, formal limousines, and the Caribbeans.

The glamorous Caribbean convertible was derived from the PanAmerican show car and was powered by a 180hp version of the faithful straight-eight engine. Although in the first year production was limited to 750 cars, the 1953 Caribbean actually outsold its arch-rival the Cadillac Eldorado, another 1953 introduction. In 1954 Packard bought out Studebaker and inherited yet more major problems, but the Caribbean line continued. In 1955 it brought out a new edition of the convertible, one of the most spectacular and lavish cars of the decade, and a true Packard in every sense.

The biggest change for Packard in 1955 was the long-overdue introduction of a V8 engine to replace the straight-eight. The straight-eight had been a great engine in its day, powerful in a smooth and lazy way, but now it was outdated; the V8 had become the industry standard. The new Packard V8 was both smooth and powerful: a 352cu in, four-barrel version, as used in the Caribbean, churned out 275 lusty

horsepower, five more than the Eldorado and far ahead of anyone else except Chrysler, who claimed 300hp in their 300, though whether Chrysler horses were as strong as Packard ones was open to conjecture. The Packard V8 was mated to a further improved version of Packard's respected Ultra-Matic transmission, which had a direct clutch as well as the usual torque convertor.

For such a large car, on a 127-inch wheelbase, the Packard was a real flier, and 1955's other innovation – Torsion-Level suspension – made it a real handler too. This was an ingenious, interlinked torsion bar system on all four wheels, with a self-levelling arrangement which allowed it automatically to compensate for all loads and surfaces. It gave the big Packard an absolutely faultless ride. The only problem for Packard was that even their impeccable engineering standards were allowed to slip in 1955. The record sales year forced the pace, and quality-control problems crept in. The new engine gained an early reputation as an oil burner and some cars quickly developed a back axle hum but,

against the overall excellence of the Caribbean, these were minor annoyances.

The Caribbean of 1955 was also, of course, a spectacularly good-looking car – long, wide and low, and with no less than three-tone paintwork. The front and tail lamps wrapped around the sides of the car, and the trim was nothing short of opulent. Later Caribbeans had reversible seat cushions, offering a choice of leather on one side or designer cloth on the other. With the price tag at $5932 the Packard was now some $300 cheaper than the latest Eldorado which, though a shadow of the 1953 car, comfortably outsold the Caribbean.

The Caribbean suffered the common problem of being widely acclaimed but left on the shelf, although eventually it became one of the most prized of collector's cars. Sadly, its excellence was not enough to save Packard. The last true Packards were built in 1956, and then Packard suffered the indignity of becoming little more than a badge-engineered Studebaker before being dragged to its demise in 1958.

SPECIFICATION

Model 1955 Packard
   Caribbean

Engine type ohv V8
Bore × stroke 4.0 × 3.5in
Capacity 352cu in
Compression ratio 8.5:1
Carburation 1 × 4bbl
Max. power 275hp
   @ 4800rpm

Transmission Ultramatic

Wheelbase 127in
Weight 4755lb

Price $5932

Preceding pages: Howard Hughes
bought this Caribbean for his
wife, Jean Peters, who promptly
parked it for the next twenty
years on the grounds that she
didn't like the colours. Most
people, including the lucky new
owner of a *very* low mileage
classic, liked the colours quite a
lot

Right: the tail pipes exit neatly
through the rear bumper corners

AT THE BEGINNING of the 1950s the sports car was not the American auto industry's strength; if you wanted a sports car you bought a European one and had people stare at you. Most of Detroit's stylists, of course, had at least some sort of love affair with the sports car, but for all the people who made appreciative noises at anything with two seats and no top, very few would dream of actually owning a sports car: it was altogether too Bohemian.

But times were changing, and buyers were becoming much more adventurous in accepting styling ideas, although they still had to have the respectability of coming from one of the Big Three. With the birth of the new generation of overhead valve V8s, status by power shared billing with status by size, and suddenly novelty was acceptable.

GM were best at gauging public amenability to new ideas. That was the purpose of their successful Motorama shows. At the 1953 Motorama, Chevrolet division showed off a fibreglass-bodied, two-seater sports car which they called the Corvette. It was decidedly European in character, tiny by American standards and simple to the point of being spartan. Its basic layout had been penned by GM technical whizz-kid Robert F. McLean and it was so small because he had abandoned the convention of starting with the front bulkhead, as was traditional, and drawing around it, and instead designed the car 'back to front' – starting at the rear axle and placing seats, bulkheads and major components as close together as possible. Harley Earl then clothed McLean's ideas in the fetching fibreglass shell and the car went to Motorama. It was a hugely successful crowd puller and was rushed straight into production. It was originally intended that only the first 300 production cars would be in fibreglass, to allow time for tooling into metal. In the event the 'glass bodies were so popular that production methods were refined and the 'vette never had metal bodywork.

In the Corvette, Chevrolet had the first mass-produced American sports car, the first post-war two-seater and the very first production car with a fibreglass body, but it was almost a failure. For a while, GM still saw the car as selling to middle America and they saw nothing wrong with the initial mix. The Corvette was introduced with a much modified 150hp version of the old 235.5cu in six and automatic transmission, and the combination was almost a disaster. With this power train the good-looking, sharp-handling little car could barely get out of its own way. In terms of performance it was in serious danger of being embarrassed by some of the big cruisers. Chevrolet adapted old Henry's ancient dictum to read 'you can have any colour you like so long as it's white (with red upholstery)' but they failed to cure the draughts and water leaks. The Corvette hardly

sold at all: 314, 3265 and 700 were the production figures for the first three season. That might have been that, except that GM kept faith and the Corvette got the V8.

The all-new 265 Chevy V8 first found its way into the Corvette in 1955, but it was really the 1956 car which saved the day. The body was restyled, borrowing equally shamelessly from the La Salle II show car and the new Mercedes 300SL, and the car was finally given the sort of performance which it looked as if it should have. The new V8 was tuned to give either 210hp with a single four-barrel carb or 225hp with the optional dual four-barrel set-up. This and 270lb ft of torque gave the 2880lb car outstanding straight-line performance. It could reach 60mph in around 7.5 seconds, 100mph in less than 20 seconds and cover a standing quarter in 15.9. In standard trim it could go two miles a minute, but as tuned (and driven) by engine wizard Zora Arkus Duntov the new V8 Corvette bettered 150mph at the 1955 Daytona Flying Mile Speed Trials.

The Corvette's spectacular new straight-line performance was only half the story. The car was already a sharp handler but new modifications were aimed, unashamedly, at making the 'vette a real racer. The light and compact new V8 contributed to an improvement in weight distribution to near-perfect front to rear balance, and changes at front and rear to castor and roll steer geometry made spectacular advances. At last the Corvette was a real sports car, demanding to be driven to the limit. It even gained a superb new three-speed manual gearbox as standard wear, with very close ratios, slick change and a crisp new coil-spring clutch. The dummy air scoops on the front fenders were now the only thing that was phoney about the little Chevy.

In 1956 Dr Dick Thompson won the SCCA Class C Production racing championship, and a Corvette driven by Crawford and Goldman won the over-3500 GT class and finished fifteenth overall in the Sebring Twelve Hours. The revitalized Corvette had just missed the boom sales year of 1955 and lost out mightily to the newly introduced Ford Thunderbird. The T'bird was slightly cheaper than the Corvette, which had rather missed the youth market owing to its fairly high price, and it was in many ways a more refined car. In 1955 it had sold more than 16,000 copies, but as Ford prepared to turn the classic Thunderbird into a dowdier four-seater, Chevrolet forged ahead.

The 'second generation' styling of the 1956 car, with its sculpted sides and aggressive grille, would change but little until the Stingray arrived in 1963. The little roadster, now in a variety of colours, grew in stature, with a bigger V8, fuel injection and gradual refinement. Now, America's only true sports car was also a seller, and the change had begun with the classic 1956 model.

SPECIFICATION

Model 1956 Chevrolet Corvette

Engine type ohv V8
Bore × stroke 3.75 × 3.0in
Capacity 265cu in
Compression ratio 9.25:1
Carburation 2 × 4bbl
Max. power 225hp @ 5200rpm

Transmission manual

Wheelbase 102in
Weight 2880lb

Price $3149

Preceding page and right: the car that put the fun back into American motoring was heading for an early demise until the much-improved 1956 version began to save the day

Above: the grille was purposeful enough, but Detroit could not resist unnecessary touches like the dummy air scoops on the front fenders

1956

In simple economic terms the Continental Mark II made no sense whatsoever. The division probably lost around $1000 on every car it made, but that was the acceptable cost of a luxury auto to upstage Cadillac and Packard. It was a money-no-object attempt to build the ultimate prestige car in the hope that some of its magic would rub off onto lesser Lincolns (which the Continental emphatically was not), where the real money was to be made.

The idea of the Continental as the symbol of leadership stemmed from the original Continental of 1941. If ever the overworked epithet 'classic' really applied, it applied to the first Continental. In 1951, a 1941 Continental Coupé had been exhibited in the Museum of Modern Art, as a work of art. It was a car loved and remembered by the public, some of the more well heeled of whom frequently asked of Lincoln 'why not another Continental?'. So Lincoln asked the question of themselves and in July 1952 a separate Continental division was set up under William Clay Ford, son of Edsel and younger brother of Henry II.

Although the original Continental had been roughly three times the price of a contemporary Ford, it was still not an expensive car compared with the best from Cadillac and Packard. When the Continental Mark II was introduced, in 1955, the average price of an American auto was $1910, so, with a basic price of around $10,000 (double the price of a Cadillac 60 Special) the Mark II was *very* expensive. It was always planned that way, priced at the very top of a market in

which Ford marketing men saw the typical Continental buyer as a fifty-one-year-old businessman with three dependents, a $50,000 home, $30,000 a year income and looking for a car to drive to his country club.

For a $10,000 car the Mark II had fairly humble beginnings, however: the first designs were rejected by Henry Ford II and the final selection was made from thirteen anonymous line drawings from various studios both inside and outside Ford. The chosen design came from the in-house Special Products Group, including Gordon Buehrig and led by John Reinhardt who had formerly been with Cadillac and Packard. The keynote was restraint; there was absolutely no need to shout about the Mark II – the smell of money would announce its arrival. The most flamboyant styling quirk was the

Above and left: in a flamboyant age, the underlying theme of the Continental Mark II was simplicity – exemplified by purity of line and straight-to-the-point instrumentation

Following pages: interior finish was exemplary and the famous spare wheel housing provided a fine billboard

SPECIFICATION

Model 1956 Continental Mark II

Engine type ohv V8
Bore × stroke 4.0 × 3.66in
Capacity 368cu in
Compression ratio 9.0:1
Carburation 1 × 4bbl
Max. power 285hp
@ 4600rpm

Transmission Multi-Drive

Wheelbase 126in
Weight 4825lb

Price $9695

much-copied 'continental' spare-wheel mounting.

Leaks of the impending launch were skilfully used to whet expensive appetites. The announcement of the car was made at a Lincoln Continental Owners Club meeting, the car was first shown in Paris, on 6 October 1955, and it was formally introduced in Dearborn fifteen days later. It was quite simply the last word in style, engineering and luxury. It was a huge, superbly built car, with no expense spared to make it right.

Assembly was painstaking in the extreme; although plenty of stock parts were used, stock assembly methods certainly were not. The body panels were first assembled for fit, then stripped, painted and reassembled. Selected engines were dyno-tested, partially dismantled, rebuilt and re-tested. Transmissions were road tested before installation. Every operation was run to extreme tolerances. Wheels, tyres and brakes were elaborately balanced before assembly, and when the car was complete it was dyno-tested again and finally road tested. On every day's production (running at around thirteen cars a day by November) the ten most common faults were identified for attention the following day. Even when the cars left the factory, in fleece-lined canvas covers, roving engineers were available to cure running problems.

The interior of the Continental Mark II offered absolutely the best materials: the finest carpets, upholstery of matched hides from Scotland, trim from single bolts of selected cloth. Every luxury except air conditioning was standard, and virtually every customer specified air as an extra. Over 200 colour combinations were offered, with almost forty trim options and, if that wasn't enough, any other choice of finish was available to order. Any requirement for special equipment would be met without question – at a price.

The Mark II was short on passenger space, shorter on luggage space, heavy on gasoline, the heaviest and most expensive car on the market. For a while customers stood in line, sometimes with dollar bills in hand, and as a result of such extraordinary demand, with growing waiting lists, some sales went to $1000 and more over list before the novelty wore off. Then, in spite of huge efforts, sales dried up. The Continental Mark II ran almost unchanged until May 1957 and was then discontinued. In eighteen months, just 3000 Mark IIs had been sold. Had Continental really known who their customers were, instead of merely thinking that they knew, they might have chased them to better effect, but there was never the remotest chance of reaching 2500 sales a year which such a loss leader needed to justify its existence and it is a near certainty that there never will be again. The Continental Mark II will remain a symbol of a magnificent attempt to build the best car in the world.

When the previously staid Chrysler Corporation discovered that it could sell performance where once it had sold respectability, there was no holding them back. By the mid 1950s, Chrysler, under the dynamic direction of Lester Colbert, who had taken over from the more conservative K.T. Keller in 1950, was abandoning its old customers in favour of what seemed to be greener pastures; by the mid-1950s each Chrysler division had its own performance car, almost invariably the model at the top end of the range, and, year by year, horsepower figures soared as the hemis went racing.

The most powerful of the Chrysler racers were the Chrysler 300 'letter-cars', introduced in 1955 and taking their name from the 300hp which the first examples produced. In 1956 the 340hp 300-B was the NASCAR Grand National Champion, Dodge was offering the D-500 performance package on any car in the Dodge range, and Plymouth was campaigning, and selling, the Fury. While Chrysler, Dodge and Plymouth did the real racing and shared the glory, De Soto had to settle for the more dubious honour of supplying the Pace Car for the 1956 Indianapolis 500. The big news for De Soto on the production car front was the mid-season introduction of the spectacular, limited-edition Adventurer.

The Adventurer was received with general acclaim, which was no bad thing, as Chrysler in general, in spite of its competition record, and De Soto in particular, needed a few public plaudits at the time; setting records and winning races was one thing, but the real object of the exercise was to sell cars, and sales were running at rock bottom. Fortunately, the 1955 De Sotos had been beautiful to look at, with some brilliant engineering detail; they were perhaps the most flamboyant of the

year's Chrysler offerings, and deservedly big sellers. Their success was opportune; in fact it probably saved the De Soto division.

The 1956 De Sotos were even better, even though they were only a cut-price face-lift of the 1955 cars. They gained some rather nicely styled fins and lost the distinctive grinning skull grille treatment, in favour of a much neater mesh design with a wide, gold anodized V motif. Whether the 1956 De Sotos looked better than the 1955 De Sotos is debatable, but they certainly looked better than most other cars.

The 1956 Adventurer revived a name first seen on a lovely Exner-styled show car of 1954, a two-door sports car built by Ghia. Had it gone into production it would have been America's first four-passenger sports car, and with the hemi-head V8 it would undoubtedly have been a car to be reckoned with. It was Exner's own favourite, a clear statement of his regard for the wheel as one of the pivotal human inventions, and not something to be hidden. The 1956 Adventurer was a very different auto from the show car but it was the top of that year's range and quite in keeping with Exner's stylistic principles. It was only available as a two-door hardtop sub-series of the 126-inch wheelbase Fireflite, although the Indy Pace Car, with Adventurer trim, was, necessarily, a convertible. The Adventurer hardtop had the most elaborate decoration, the best trim and the most

horsepower – 320 at 5200rpm, from 341cu in – of the year's De Sotos. De Soto were the masters of spectacular paintwork, and the Adventurer combined vivid colours with anodized, gold-plated brightwork, such as the grille, nameplates and the unique, spoked wheelcovers. Luxurious leather or leather and nylon seats were colour keyed to the exterior, and the Adventurer generally exuded style.

It was the most expensive De Soto to date, at $3728 roughly on a par with the Chrysler New Yorker. Five hundred Adventurers (the planned extent of the edition) were sold in 1956, which was a good year for De Soto in a mediocre year for Chrysler as a whole. The Adventurer name continued for as long as the marque survived, until 1961, and it graced some fast, finely styled cars, but none better than the original.

Through the 1950s De Soto had something of an identity problem; at the same time as the division was building some of its best ever cars it was inexorably going out of business. Most of the damage was done not by mistakes or shortcomings on De Soto's part but by seemingly logical changes in Chrysler's corporate marketing structure, inadvertently bringing De Soto into more and more damaging conflict with the cheaper Dodge lines. Dodge survived the encounter, De Soto didn't; there was little more logic to it than that, and little more justice.

SPECIFICATION

Model 1956 De Soto
     Adventurer

Engine type ohv V8
Bore × stroke 3.72 × 3.80in
Capacity 341.4cu in
Compression ratio 9.25:1
Carburation 1 × 4bbl
Max. power 320hp
     @ 5200rpm

Transmission PowerFlite

Wheelbase 126in
Weight 3870lb

Price $3728

Preceding pages, left and far left: the limited edition Adventurer, like many earlier De Sotos, was both stylish and beautifully equipped, but cars like this were not enough to overcome the division's identity problems and for De Soto the end was near

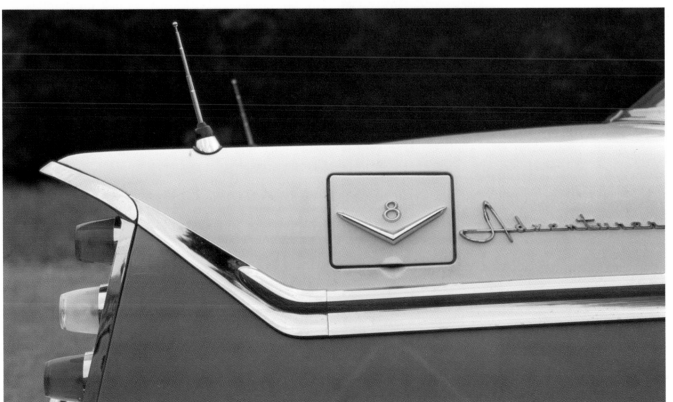

Thunderbird

To the north american Indians of the eastern forests and the Great Plains, Thunderbirds were enormous birds with huge wings and human faces, which lived above the sky between earth and heaven. They were symbols of power and a link with the gods. The beat of their wings made the thunder, and the fierce flashing of their eyes was the lightning. In 1953 there was a certain amount of thunder and lightning around Detroit too, when General Motors discovered that Ford had just beaten them to the post in registering Thunderbird as a model name. It was a perfect name for a sports car, and a sports car was what the Thunderbird was originally intended to be.

In the early 1950s Ford were climbing out of their desperate straits of 1946; Henry II was picking up the pieces left by his grandfather, and Lewis D. Crusoe was Vice President and General Manager of the Ford division. In 1951 Crusoe and his assistant, freelance designer George Walker, were at the Paris Salon. Crusoe saw Jaguars, Porsches and Ferraris and he saw an all-American sports car as the image- and prestige-booster Ford desperately needed. Walker saw a lucrative design project and called his office to say so; by

the time the two returned, outlines were laid. By February 1953 there was a commitment in principle to the car and in September of the same year, in the light of the appearance of the Corvette, the final go-ahead was given by Crusoe, again calling from Paris, for a two-seater sports car.

The original brief was for a car weighing around 2500lb, V8-powered, capable of exceeding 100mph, and with two seats and a canvas top. It was to utilize as many off-the-shelf Ford components as possible, which was no doubt some relief to Bob Maguire's studio, which was given three months to prepare the first mock-ups. The first presentations were actually full-sized, air-brushed cut-outs – there was no time for models – and from the start the emphasis was on straight-cut styling. At the time stylists at Ford were secondary to engineers, but for the Thunderbird they were adamant that they did not simply want to clothe a shortened sedan chassis; they wanted to start with the engine lower and further back than the American norm and, because of the unusual enthusiasm surrounding the car, they were given what they wanted.

As a result of the rush, the Thunderbird was thoroughly over-engineered. The cross-braced frame could rely on almost no help from the body, which had little or no inherent stiffness – in fact, the rear wheel covers were added principally because the depth of the original fender looked absurd. The hood scoop, for once, was strictly functional, to accommodate the carb, and the attractive rear lights were a fortuitous spin-off from the 1955 range. Of necessity, the running tests were in fact done on a shortened sedan chassis and resulted in softer then standard front coil springs and shorter rear leafs. The front brakes were slightly down-graded to ease premature locking.

The first prototype was already around 350 pounds over the target weight, and in the winter of 1953–4 Crusoe decided to transform the car from a straightforward sports car to a more luxurious 'personal' car, with power brakes, steering, seats and windows, and a hardtop option. The shortcomings of the early Corvettes had not gone unnoticed, and to reach a production target of 10,000 a year Ford needed something special. The first production cars weighed around 3200lb.

The first car left the lines on 9 September 1954. The model was formally announced on 23 September and went on sale on 26 October at a basic price of $2695, which included the lift-off hardtop and power seats but did not include the optional soft top. Bodies were made by Budd, then trimmed and painted at Dearborn, and were almost totally free of unnecessary ornament. It was a beautiful car and sold well, as did almost everything else in the industry's record year.

The 1956 Thunderbird was the classic two-seater. Learning from the lessons of introduction year, it changed but little. The biggest visual differences were a 'continental' spare wheel location (for this year only), optional portholes in the rear quarters of the hardtop for better visibility, and swivelling front vent windows for better ventilation. The last two were successful modifications (four out of five buyers took the portholes, for example) but the 'continental' spare paid for its rakish looks and slight improvement in trunk space by making luggage access and wheel changing difficult. Twelve-volt electrics were another main advance.

Strangely, although most of the weight that the car gained for 1956 was behind the rear axle and the steering ratio was reduced, it was a better handler than models of previous years. This must have been due to a softening of the rear springs and the fact that the quick-response steering of the 1955 was sharp almost to the point of being jerky. The 1956 Thunderbird also gained some front-end weight by virtue of a slightly heavier engine, so the distribution was still not far short of ideal.

The 1956 Thunderbird was on a par with the original in terms of performance, making up for the extra weight with more horsepower from the standard 292 or optional 312cu in motors. It could reach 60mph from rest in around 9½ seconds and had a top speed of perhaps 115mph. That was a far cry from the Corvette, but so were Thunderbird sales; although for 1956 they were down to 15,631, Corvette sold less than 5000.

Unfortunately, Ford didn't know when to stay with a good thing, and after only one more year as a two-seater the Thunderbird grew into an unsuccessful dressed-up four-seater which no self-respecting Indian would have been seen dead worshipping. It was a sad loss.

Preceding pages and left: there wasn't too much wrong with the early, two-seater Thunderbird formula, especially with the 1956 refinements, but Ford changed from this good thing just a year later

Above: the symbol of power

Model 1956 Thunderbird

Engine type ohv V8
Bore × stroke 3.75 × 3.3in
Capacity 292cu in
Compression ratio 8.4:1
Carburation 1 × 4bbl
Max. power 202hp
@ 4600rpm

Transmission manual

Wheelbase 102in
Weight 3308lb

Price $3155

THE DICTIONARY DEFINITION of a brougham, pronounced bro-erm or broom, is that it is a one-horse close carriage or a motor car with uncovered driver's seat. The 1957 Cadillac Eldorado Brougham was neither. Its driver, like the rest of its occupants, was cocooned in the utmost luxury and in place of one horse it offered around 325hp. It did, nevertheless, have a certain style which may not have been wasted on the eponymous Lord Brougham, had he not missed the car by almost a century.

Like many of GM's best cars, the Eldorado Brougham took its first bow at Motorama, in this case at the 1955 show, although it could also trace its ancestry to the Orleans and Park Avenue show cars of the two preceding years. The Orleans had been a relatively conservative design, but it had shown that it was possible to combine a wraparound windshield with four-door hardtop styling. The Park Avenue was a pillared four-door but it was topped by a roof of brushed aluminium. For 1955, spurred by public enthusiasm for these cars, Harley Earl had combined the best of both and rolled out the first Eldorado Brougham. The new car was finished in January, just two days before the New York Motorama, and was only rescued for the public gaze by frantic panel beating after it had fallen from its perch just hours before the doors opened.

Cadillac did not need to worry unduly about such upstarts as the soon-to-be-revived Continental; the Standard of the World remained the car to aspire to. More to the point was that even Cadillac had to pander to a market beyond the merely exclusive: they were a privileged few who could add such a sybaritic wonder as the Brougham to their possessions and not flinch at the price. Even in the land of opportunity there were not many such fortunates to be found but, with the chance to start the bidding on Eldorado Broughams at over $13,000, there were enough to keep Cadillac happy. Meanwhile, the other major luxury builders, Lincoln and Imperial, could squabble amongst themselves over who picked up second place.

Like the 1955 show car, the (very) limited edition 1957 Eldorado Brougham, which was actually introduced in December 1956, was a pillarless, four-door four-seater, with brushed stainless-steel roof, although it had undergone quite a few styling changes from the original look. The expected Cadillac mechanical excellence was based in this case on an all-new, stiffer and lower, tubular, cruciform frame, without side rails. It was the smallest chassis of Cadillac's twelve-model 1957 range and the Brougham stood only four-and-a-half feet high. It had the traditional Cadillac 'V' emblem and egg-crate grille, but its quad headlights were revolutionary for a GM car.

The Brougham used the refined and potent 365cu in

Cadillac Eldorado Brougham Coupé

SPECIFICATION

Model 1957 Cadillac
Eldorado Brougham

Engine type ohv V8
Bore × stroke 4.0 × 3.625in
Capacity 365cu in
Compression ratio 10.0:1
Carburation 1 × 4bbl
Max. power 325hp
@ 4800rpm

Transmission Hydra-Matic

Wheelbase 129.5in
Weight 5152lb

Price $13,074

Preceding pages and right: as fins, quite literally, approached their peak, the originators had some of their finest. The handsome Eldorado Brougham was a very practical spin-off from GM's thought-provoking Motorama show cars, combining four-door hardtop styling with imaginative use of materials – as on the brushed stainless steel roof

Inset, right: completely pillarless construction gave suitably dignified access to a sumptuous interior

V8, whose compression ratio now reached double figures for the first time, and this accounted for the 325 horses to be delivered through the old faithful Hydra-Matic. Undaunted by problems encountered with similar systems on more mundane cars, GM treated the Cadillac to an air suspension system, which promised superior ride comfort with self-levelling and load-adjusting capabilities and the facility to raise ride height or jack the car at the touch of a switch. The system differed from others in that the compressor which fed the reserve tank and the diaphragmed wheel cylinders breathed from the atmosphere rather than being closed. It did not differ from the others in being prone to leaks, however, and was eventually dropped after four frustrating years. While it was working properly, of course, the air suspension gave the Brougham a near-faultless ride, totally in keeping with the general level of refinement.

Cadillac management had always aspired to building 'the finest car possible' and the ultimate judges were to be the people who rode in it. The Eldorado Brougham did not really offer options; everything was standard equipment, including individually controllable front and rear heating, polarized sun visors, signal-seeking radio and a range of vanity equipment that would not have been out of place in a beauty parlour. The Eldorado Brougham also had an automatic speed control which was in effect the forerunner of cruise control. It had powered everything, not only the brakes and steering but also the seats, which had multi-directional power adjustment with 'memory' settings to return them to favourite positions. The window lifts were powered and so was the trunk lid which, at the touch of a dashboard switch, would glide quietly up and down with the help of an electric motor. Only air conditioning was considered an option on the Brougham. On a lesser car, all these gadgets might have been considered mere gimmickry, but on the hand-built Cadillac they were functional, reliable and more or less to be taken for granted.

Just 400 Eldorado Broughams were built in the first model year, and that tiny output was to represent the highest number of Eldorado Broughams in any year of its four-year run. In 1958, 304 cars were built, and the car was little changed and still clothed by Fleetwood. The following year the car was completely restyled and the bodywork entrusted to Pininfarina in Turin, one of the most respected of all the European coachbuilding houses. Unfortunately the Pininfarina-built Eldorado Broughams were not in the same league as the Detroit-built cars, either in terms of styling (done in Detroit) or in production quality. Sales plummeted to 200 in two years and heralded the end of another milestone, the magnificent, made-in-Detroit 1957 Eldorado Brougham.

Chevrolet Bel Air Hardtop

THE 1957 CHEVROLET BEL AIR is the definitive evocation of mid-1950s young America, ranking with rock and roll, hula hoops, drive-in movies and Davy Crockett hats as a cherished reminder of the era. The 1957 Chevrolet was loved then because it was stylish, solid, sporty and cheap. It is loved now because it is just as stylish, solid and sporty, with the added ingredient of nostalgia. It is no longer cheap, of course, because it ranks as one of the most collectable of American autos.

The 1957 Chevys really originated in 1955, with a road-to-roof redesign of the old line. The styling was recognizably Chevrolet, but so simple and well balanced that the design was immediately acknowledged as a classic. It underwent minor improvements in 1956 and again for 1957 and, bucking the trend, lost barely a trace of its original elegance in the process, in spite of sprouting slightly larger fins, a bigger grille and bumpers, and anodized rear fender panels. The Bel Air was top of the three non-Corvette ranges and came as sedan, hardtop, convertible and the pretty Nomad hardtop wagon. All were perfectly proportioned, finely detailed and almost totally devoid of the usual contemporary brashness, the only minor blemish being 'bombsights' on the hood; that aside, the 1957 Bel Air is one of the most handsome of post-war American autos.

It was also more, much more, than a pretty face. Along with the new looks, 1955 had brought a new motor, Ed Cole's milestone 265cu in V8, which was one of the finest American engines ever made. Extremely light, compact and strong, it was even lighter than the six which it supplemented, a mere 22 inches long and capable of an enormous amount of tuning. For 1957 there was a bigger bore, 283cu in version of the already well over square 'small block'. It was available in a range of horsepowers from 185 to 283 – the magic equivalent of one horsepower per cubic inch, never before seen from a mass-produced American auto engine. This 'Super Turbo-Fire 283' produced its 283hp at 6200rpm, with the help of 'Ramjet' continuous flow fuel injection – from GM's Rochester division. It was another first, the first time that injection had been offered on a production car. This alternative to four-barrel carburation as the top option not only boosted top end power but it also gave better throttle response and eliminated surge-induced fuel starvation, which could be a particularly embarrassing problem, for instance, when it caused the engine to stutter in extreme cornering attitudes. With any of the optional 283 engines (the six and the latest version of the 265, rated at 162hp were also available), the compact and relatively light Bel Air was a snappy performer – or, as Chevrolet put it, 'Sweet, Smooth and Sassy'.

The range of transmission options included a three-speed manual (the best choice for outright performance), Overdrive, Powerglide, or the latest, triple turbine, Turboglide. Turboglide was another excellent GM auto, offering infinitely variable torque multiplication from standstill to cruising speed and having a low ratio selector called the 'Hill Retarder' for increased engine braking. It took full advantage of the V8's smooth and ample torque and power curves, and a 1957 Bel Air with the 270hp motor, for example, would run 0–60mph in around 9½ seconds, comfortably top

Model 1957 Chevrolet Bel-
Air hardtop

Engine type ohv V8
Bore × stroke 3.875 × 3.0in
Capacity 283cu in
Compression ratio 10.5:1
Carburation fuel injection
Max. power 283hp
@ 6200rpm

Transmission manual

Wheelbase 115in
Weight 3296lb

Price $2464

Above: the first American production engine to give one horsepower per cubic inch – the fuel-injected Chevy 283

Right and inset, right: aside from the completely superfluous bombsights on the hood, Bel Air styling was a paragon of good taste

Preceding pages: functional air scoops around the headlights duct air to the engine compartment

110mph and turn a 17½-second quarter mile. Since 1955 it had been the hot-rodder's, drag-strip and street-racer's favourite; it was strong, reliable and capable of an amazing amount of tuning and customizing without spending a huge amount.

From the beginning, the new Chevrolet also distinguished itself at the Daytona Speed Weeks, with speeds up to 131mph, and in NASCAR short-track racing; Chevys won over half of the 1955 short-track events. Chevy tuning wizard Zora Arkus Duntov shattered the twenty-one-year-old stock car record at Pikes Peak hill climb with a 1956 model, and Chevrolet easily won the Pure Oil Trophy at Daytona in 1957 for the best overall performances. These included the first three places in the smaller stock class and almost every place in the 305cu in division. It was to be something of a swansong for the competition Chevys, at least so far as the factory entries were concerned, because 1957 brought a 'recommendation' from the Automobile Manufacturers Association to end participation in racing henceforth. In fact, this might have been something of a face-saver for Chevrolet, as the 1958 redesign brought big, soft cars quite different from the sharp 1957s in performance terms.

Chevy's defeat of Ford at the 1957 Speed Weeks was not repeated in the market-place, although it was a very close run thing, with a mere handful of sales separating the rivals in the final reckoning. Plagued by material shortages in the factories and hit by the success of Exner's restyled Plymouths and some very good new Fords, Chevrolet lost the number one slot to the latter. It was about the only flaw in the 1957 cars' catalogue. The words of a country song sum it up nicely: 'They don't make cars like they used to, I wish we still had it today; the love that we found, the good love that we're living, we owe it to that old '57 Chevrolet'.

THE 1950S SAW SOME big changes at Chrysler, many of them for the better, but it was no easy route that led from the mostly dowdy 1950 models to the stunningly styled 1957 'Forward Look' Chrysler New Yorker.

The key to the emergence of the acclaimed Chrysler styling of the mid- and late-1950s was Virgil Exner, who joined the corporation in 1949, from Studebaker. Exner and Harley Earl, of General Motors, rank as the two major contributors to American automobile styling since styling became the most important word in the industry. Arriving at Chrysler after breaking with Raymond Loewy over the design of the Studebaker Starliner, Exner inherited designs owing more to engineering than to aesthetics, and with them the sales problems that such emphasis then implied. Chrysler sales continued to sink perilously low before Exner had the opportunity of a complete redesign; in the meantime the marque survived largely on its reputation for sound engineering, reliability and performance.

It was not until 1955 that Exner's influence made its first real impact, with the arrival of the 'Hundred Million Dollar Look', from which the 1957 shape evolved; and sales immediately began to climb out of the depths. The 1955s, and even prettier 1956s, probably didn't earn the corporation quite a hundred million dollars, but they did pay for the 1957 'Forward Look'.

Exner's taste was for simple, rakish lines, embodied (except for some very silly rear light treatments) in earlier Chrysler show cars such as the Ghia-built K-310 of 1951. His 1957 models were probably the best production examples of his design philosophy: they were simply beautiful. They were big cars but, because they followed Exner's creed of conceiving the car first as a whole, they did not appear bulky or inelegant.

The Forward Look seriously alarmed Chrysler's competitors, especially GM and Earl, who reacted to its success by producing disastrously overblown responses for 1958. Exner's 1957 cars had clean, sharp fins and, unlike those of the 1956 cars, they were integral with the body rather than grafted on to it. The Forward Look also included the novelty of compound-curve windshields and the option of dual headlights on all models. The New Yorker was second only to the immensely fast 300-C at the top of the 1957 range, and although it shared its 126-inch wheelbase and all body panels with the rest of the range, it was distinguished by side trims, colour matched to the roof, and seven totally superfluous trim 'teeth' on the rear fenders. The new styling was quite rightly much acclaimed, and awarded two Grands Prix d'Honneur and two Gold Medals by the Industrial Designers' Institute.

The panic amongst the competition was also due to the New Yorker's mechanical specification, which was a further reflection of the sporty image engendered by

cars such as the 300 'lettercars'. Chrysler's 392cu in V8 was the biggest production engine of the year, up to this capacity for the first time as a result of increases in both bore and stroke. Notwithstanding cubic inches, this was in any event one of the most respected engines: the hemi-head Fire Power. It was efficient, while able to run on low-octane gasoline, and capable of staggering outputs. In the 1957 New Yorker the big hemi ran up to 325hp at 4600rpm. The 300-C versions were good for as much as 390hp and in future years, with supercharging and running with nitro fuels, hemis prepared for drag racing would approach 2000hp.

Part of its ability to stay on the road even under the influence of so much horsepower lay in Chrysler's new suspension system, which was the final secret ingredient of the sensational 1957 mixture. This was Torsion-Aire, a genuine step forward in suspension systems, which gave both ride and handling. Torsion bars were not new but they were certainly a novelty on

SPECIFICATION

Model 1957 Chrysler New Yorker convertible

Engine type ohv V8
Bore × stroke 4.0 × 3.9in
Capacity 392cu in
Compression ratio 9.25:1
Carburation 1 × 4bbl
Max. power 325hp
@ 4600rpm

Transmission PowerFlite

Wheelbase 126in
Weight 4365lb

Price $4638

Preceding page, above and right: the sweeping lines of Virgil Exner's 1957 'Forward Look' styling set Chrysler models apart from the crowd, at a time when many other stylists were struggling to find a way to build big *and* beautiful. Aside from a little overdecoration, Exner's designs were beautifully clean and sharp

cars in the New Yorker's price range. The longitudinal torsion bars were used only on the front of the car, in place of the more usual coil springs. They offered more progressive springing rates, particularly under severe usage, and quite exceptional handling for the time.

The year 1957 was crucial for the performance image, the final year in which the Automobile Manufacturers' Association was to approve, grudgingly, of factory competition involvement. Chrysler's performance image was right for the moment and it sold a lot of cars, taking the marque back into the top ten. Unfortunately Chrysler had made essential economies by losing engineering staff and financial controllers; production quality of the otherwise excellent cars was poor and productivity was worse; and in the recession year of 1958 that spelt disaster. It was a very sad end for some of the best cars Chrysler ever made.

1957

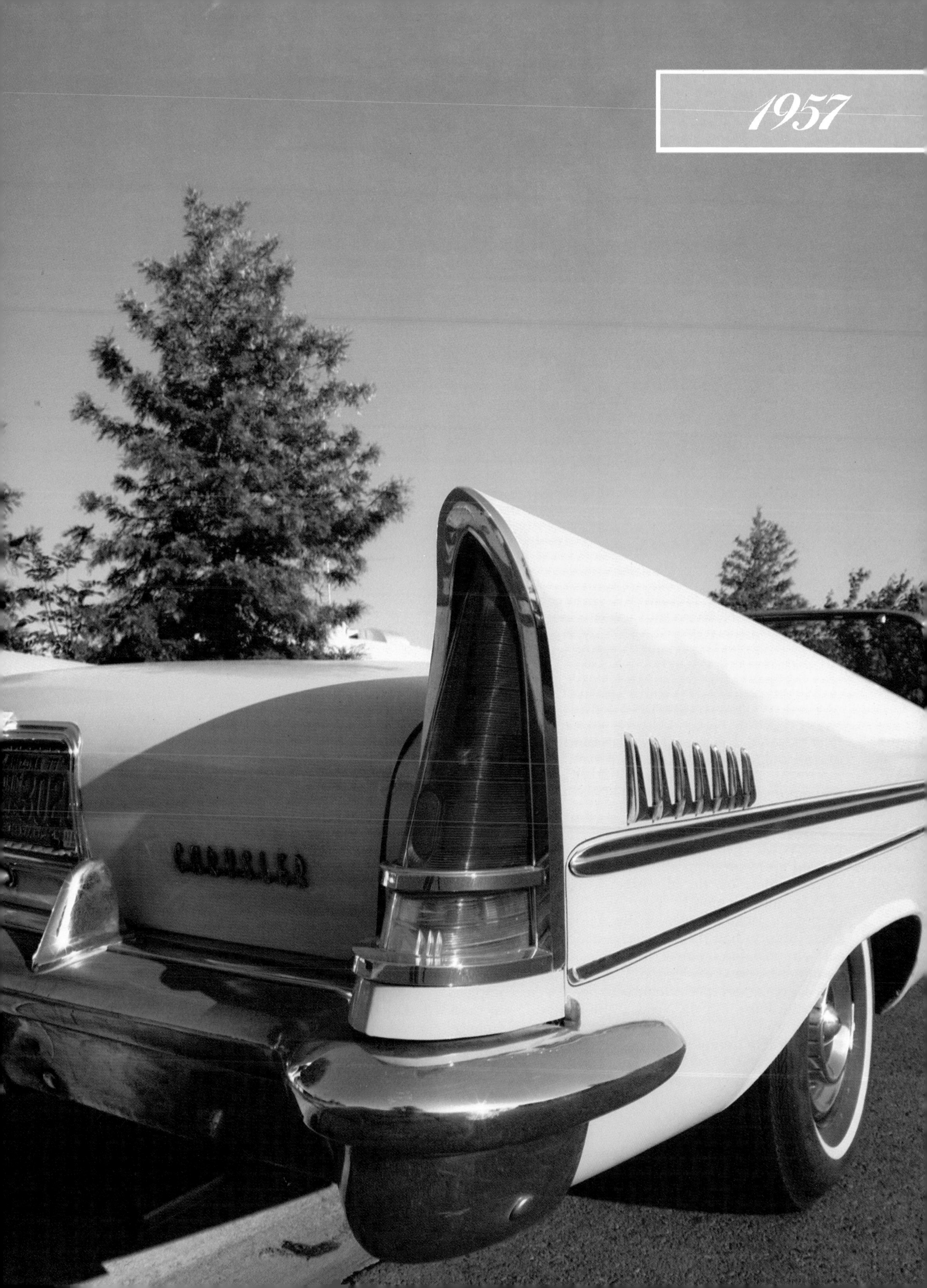

'STEP INTO THE Wonderful World of AUTODYNAMICS!' yelled the ads for the 1957 Dodge range. 'It is Swept Wing Mastery of Motion. It Unleashes a Hurricane of Power. It Tames a Tornado of Torque. It Breaks Through the Vibration Barrier' – and so it went on. Fortunately the cars were a little more subtle than the ads, as was to be expected since they came largely from the drawing board of Virgil Exner and his team.

Leading Dodge's offerings was the Custom Royal Lancer, in hardtop and convertible guises, which was just what the ad-men ordered. The 'Wonderful World of AUTODYNAMICS', 1957-style, was the wonderful world of 'big is beautiful'. Still intoxicated by memories of 1955, the industry was going collectively overboard to offer more of everything: bigger bodies, better trim, more dress-up options and more gaudy looks. Just being better was no good unless you were seen to be better, so cars like the Custom Royal Lancer were doing their bit for style by size.

Like all the 1957 Dodges (and some of their sister Plymouths and De Sotos) the Custom Royal sat on a 122-inch wheelbase; it was over 17½ feet long and 6½ feet wide, but not so gross as most, thanks largely to Exner's touch. 'Forward Look' was what Chrysler called the new corporate style for 1957, and what Madison Avenue called 'Swept Wing Mastery of Motion'. The tail fins were big because everyone else's new tail fins were big, and getting bigger, but they were stylishly simple – they never did get really out of hand at Dodge. The overall look was meant to be purposeful and aggressive, not trashy, and it succeeded. The Custom Royal Lancers had more decoration than the cheaper Dodges, but were smoothly styled and powerful looking.

Since the 1951 introduction of the potent hemi, performance had been Chrysler's forte, which was backed up by an extraordinary record of racing success in the mid-1950s, for the three divisions of Chrysler, Dodge and Plymouth. Even on the race track the corporate pecking order of the market-place applied. Each division had its own performance leader and the top optional horsepower figures read Plymouth 290, Dodge 310 and Chrysler 390. While the 1957 Plymouth and Chrysler top-performance options were complete cars (the Fury and the 300-C), the Dodge D-500 (and even more powerful D500-1) option was a performance kit applicable to any model in the range, including the well-appointed Custom Royal Lancers. The optional power was not cheap and the D-500 Dodges were gas guzzlers, but to the agency they were 'snarling, aircraft type super Red Ram V8s'.

NASCAR and USAC late model stock car racing was big business for the factories through 1956 and 1957, and Dodges (and others) became the better for it. With the 'ordinary' 260hp, 325cu in V8, the Custom Royal

was quite a mover; with the 354cu in, D-500-1 V8, dual four-barrel carbs and 340hp, it was dynamite – if only in a 'point and squirt' sort of way. Tearing off twenty-second dashes to 100mph was what cars like the D-500 equipped Dodges were all about.

The new chassis with smaller diameter wheels and ball-joint suspension was fine, and the uprated front Torsion-Aire torsion-bar suspension, stiffer rear springs, stiffer shocks and uprated brakes that went with the big motor put the D-500 equipped Royals near the best for handling, but cars like this were really too big to be in the sports car league. The industry's biggest brake pedal and (actually quite good) Total Contact, Anti-Dive brakes were still not enough to tame 340 horses; a certain amount of circumspection, a helping of road sense and no small degree of skill were needed too.

Even with the Dodge, which was a lot better than some of the other overpowered, under-engineered street-racers, many kids found that out the hard way, the first time they ran out of straight road.

The 'muscle' cars would be around a while longer and they would earn some valid criticism, but, sadly, 1957 was the swansong for the trend-setting hemi. It was replaced by the bigger, less efficient but cheaper wedge-head V8s. As the horsepower race continued, Detroit was forced to de-emphasize competition and performance, leaving Madison Avenue to wring what excitement it could from recessed door handles, transistor radios which tuned automatically to the strongest local station, and from seat materials called Silver Strata, Linear Lucidity and Gotham Texture. Batman, eat your heart out.

Model 1957 Dodge Custom
 Royal Lancer

Engine type ohv V8
Bore × stroke 3.69 × 3.8in
Capacity 325cu in
Compression ratio 8.5:1
Carburation 1 × 4bbl
Max. power 260hp
 @ 4400rpm

Transmission PowerFlite

Wheelbase 122in
Weight 3690lb

Price $2881

Pages 84–5: Dodge's version of
the 1957 Chrysler restyling
programme was 'Swept Wing'
styling with fins overlapping the
rear fenders and masses of
brightwork. The Custom Royal
Lancer was the most elaborately
decorated of all the middle-
market Dodge offerings for 1957

Left: the beautiful sweeping
roofline of the hardtop

Right: rocket influence was never
far away during the later part of
the decade

OF ALL THE weird and wonderful devices which the American auto industry spawned in the flamboyant 1950s, the 1957 Ford Fairlane 500 Skyliner, the first and last mass-produced retractable hardtop, was surely the weirdest. The paying public loved convertibles, but they didn't like the difficulties associated with a soft top; they liked a steel roof, but they also loved the sun in their faces and the wind in their hair. The Ford Motor Company lived as far as possible by the adage 'give the people what they want' – and if what the people wanted was a hardtop that hid in the trunk, then that was what they would have.

The idea itself was not new: in 1940 Le Baron had built half-a-dozen stunning show cars for Chrysler, designed by Alex Tremulis and Ralph Roberts, and called the Thunderbolt. These had a tiny hardtop which, by the operation of a series of switches, could be juggled into the trunk space, to leave a smooth, open two-seater. Seventeen years later, the Skyliner offered a full-sized hardtop which did exactly the same trick at the touch of a button, and in the first five months of production it attracted 20,766 customers.

The Ford retractable should actually have been a Lincoln retractable; the $2.2 million project to design the top, conceived by Gil Spear and started in July 1953, had originally been intended for the forthcoming Continental Mark II, but then Ford realized that the sort of numbers in which the $10,000 Continental could sell would never recover the top's tooling costs. It just so happened that the trunk-to-passenger-space proportions of the embryo Fairlane were the same, so the Mark II was taken to the Ford studio and hurriedly restyled from the waist down, to become the Fairlane Skyliner. This was not such a major operation as it might sound: the top and trunk spaces dictated virtually all else, and in any case the car had to be a recognizable part of the family.

The 1957 Fords harked back to a show car called the Mystere, which was built for 1954 but never shown because it was too close to the 1957 plans. The Skyliner (whose name carried over from the earlier, fixed perspex-roof models of 1954 to 1956) was first shown, in prototype form, at the New York Auto Show in December 1956. There and elsewhere it was well received, and Ford made the most of the public's anticipation by delaying its official introduction by a couple of months after the rest of the range. The first production model was actually presented to President Eisenhower, on 14 April 1957, and at the time he probably wished the rest of his problems would disappear as smoothly as the Skyliner's top did. The new Fairlane was supposedly a mid-size car, but it was big by any standards, with a 118-inch wheelbase and an overall length of 17½ feet. It was the first of the long,

low Fords and also introduced swept rear wings, sculpted side panels and the huge, round rear lights which were to become a modern Ford trademark. It was intended to help Ford break into the middle-price market where its share was a lamentable thirteen-and-a-half-per-cent, and to a large extent it succeeded.

Given the complexity of the whole mechanism, it is a great credit to the design team that the idea worked as well as it undeniably did. The top, counterbalanced by huge springs across the floor of the trunk, had three drive motors, four locking motors, ten power relays, eight circuit-breakers, ten cut-off switches and over 600 feet of wiring – all actuated by a single switch which triggered a sequence of actions which never failed to amaze. With the transmission in Park (this was *not* a trick to perform while moving) and with or without the motor running, a click of the switch first caused the rear deck locks to open and the trunk lid to open, on rear hinges and via screw jacks. Next, the rear tray extended to bridge the gap to the rear seat, then the joints from the roof to the windshield and the roof to the rear quarters unlocked and the top began its journey. After it had partly retracted it stopped, to allow the first ten-inch segment to fold under – a necessary concomitant of fitting 90 inches of roof into 84 inches of trunk. When the folded top had stowed itself, the lid came down and locked and that was that – all in around one minute. As the operation was sequential, any stop meant all stop and there were comprehensive trouble-shooting instructions with each car, as well as an extremely slow manual back-up, but these were seldom needed.

Mechanically, the Skyliner was in other respects just another Ford. The 292cu in V8 was standard, but the 312cu in, 245hp option was usually taken, along with the 'improved' two-speed Fordomatic transmission, which was only slightly less tacky than the original. It had a very stiff, heavily cross-braced chassis and ball-joint front suspension, with a clever variable-rate system on the rear leaf springs, but it was certainly no sports car when it came to handling. There were the usual quality-control problems and the cars were prone to rust but, aside from a tendency to metal fatigue in the top itself (cured by the addition of rather inelegant ribbing for 1958), the retractable was thoroughly reliable, if not completely practical. It had less leg room than the hardtop but was on a par with the soft top and actually quite roomy; the big problem was that, with the hood stowed, the only usable trunk space was an inaccessible 30 × 24 × 15-inch box in the middle of the trunk and on top of the spare wheel.

The retractable was jazzed up for 1958 but sales fell; for 1959 it became the attractive Galaxie and sales fell further; for 1960 it was no more. The novelty had worn off, and by then Ford had had a better idea.

Model Ford Fairlane 500
   Skyliner

Engine type ohv V8
Bore × stroke 3.75 × 3.30in
Capacity 292cu in
Compression ratio 9.0:1
Carburation 1 × 2bbl
Max. power 212hp
   @ 4200rpm

Transmission Fordomatic

Wheelbase 118in
Weight 3916lb

Price $3138

Pages 88–9: with the top either up
or down the Fairlane 500 Skyliner
looked innocuous enough,
but. . . .

Left: . . . . something very strange
happened in between – all at the
touch of a button

Inset, below left: with the roof
stowed in the trunk, luggage
space (the box in the middle) was
strictly in the toothbrush and tie
league

WHEN IS A Chrysler not a Chrysler? Answer: when it's an Imperial. Until 1955 Imperial was no more than an up-market Chrysler model name, but then, in an attempt to overcome an unwanted image as 'just another Chrysler', Imperial became a separate marque. In fact, the ploy was not a great success and Imperial always remained cast in the Chrysler mould, being repatriated officially in 1975. Meanwhile, Imperial cars had some of their best-ever sales years and the division built some of its best-ever models, including the 1957 Imperial Crown.

During its first couple of years as an ostensibly separate marque, Imperial was largely content to rest on the laurels of the beautifully built, Exner-styled Newports, but the corporation bosses expected more than that from their exclusive offshoot. The upgrading of the Imperial range in 1957 was a direct challenge to Lincoln for second place in the lucrative luxury-car sector – Cadillac being acknowledged as the unassailable leader.

In 1957 LeBaron and Imperial Crown joined Imperial, as premium series. The Le Baron came in sedan and four-door hardtop guises and the Crown as sedan, convertible and two- and four-door hardtops, this year's convertible being the first since the marque became a separate entity. The 1957 Imperials were quite different from the other 1957 Chryslers. They were built on a 129-inch wheelbase chassis, which was four inches shorter than the previous year's Imperials but still three inches longer than the 'ordinary' Chryslers. Status by size was all-important, and Imperial continued to use the same 129-inch wheelbase until 1966. In spite of the size difference, the Imperials were recognizably part of Virgil Exner's corporate 'Forward Look', widely acclaimed as a real step forward in styling.

To pretend to the luxury car throne it was necessary to be a little bit ostentatious, as well as simply being big. Where the 1957 Chryslers had a relatively plain front-end treatment, the Imperial Crown was very glittery. The grille was full width, quite elaborate and just dripping with chrome. Below was a wraparound, two-tier bumper and above were exaggerated hoods for the protruding dual headlights, (in fact, only the Crown hardtops had dual headlights; the sedans somehow had to make do with just one pair.) The 'eyebrows' were neatly finished with chrome edges and stylized golden crown badges; their line ran smoothly into the uncluttered body line, pointing gracefully back to the leading edges of the huge fins. The fins were basically very clean but each housed a bullet-shaped tail-lamp with a rather unnecessary chrome collar. The Imperial name was writ large on each flank in chrome script, above a tapering side spear.

These Imperial Crown hardtops had a very

Imperial Crown

Preceding pages: Imperial's rather attractive variation on the 'continental' spare wheel location was much better for looks than for luggage space

Above and top: Exner's 'Forward Look' certainly produced some handsome cars

Right: luxury buyers expected a few extras, like dual headlights, two-tier bumpers and masses of chrome

distinctive, chevron-stepped roofline, finished in two colours, and an equally distinctive tail-end treatment. The sharply sloping trunk lid housed the spare wheel, not exactly Continental-style, but at least raised up for all to see. It looked quite pretty but did nothing at all for the luggage space.

As well as being very good-looking cars, the Imperial Crowns were naturally beautifully finished and furnished, even more so in fact than the basic Imperials. A variety of seat and trim combinations in leather and cloth was available and the interiors were light and roomy.

By this time, Chrysler were widely acknowledged for their excellent engines, transmission and suspension – largely as a result of the corporation's competition interests. All the 1957 Imperials shared similar running gear. They were all powered by the 392cu in hemi, producing some 325hp and driving through a three-speed TorqueFlite automatic, with push-button selection. Although they were obviously fairly heavy cars (typically weighing over two tons, thanks to luxury trim and equipment) they were no sluggards, and they were surprisingly frugal on gasoline.

In 1957, for the first and what would be the only time in its short history, Imperial achieved its ambition and outsold Lincoln. In spite of the looming recession, Imperial managed to sell 37,946 cars, including just thirty-six memorable editions of the top-of-the-line limousine range, the Ghia Crown Imperial. This was essentially an Imperial two-door hardtop with over 20in added to the wheel-base, and finished to the utmost standards of luxury by Ghia in Turin. This 1957 sales figure of thirty-six cars was its best ever – perhaps predictably, as prices started at around $15,000.

Imperials were almost all good, interesting autos, but they suffered from an identity problem. Very few buyers below the level of the magnates and potentates who bought the Ghia Crowns could set aside the thought that the Imperial was but a jollied-up Chrysler, whereas a Cadillac was a Cadillac was a Cadillac – and there was little difference in price. Imperial was probably much more at home when it was welcomed back into the Chrysler fold in the 1970s.

In 1957 ANOTHER recession was fast approaching in the USA and car sales were falling, but that was no reason for not having something new to offer. Most of 1957's new models had of course been in the pipeline at least since the boom year of 1955, when manufacturers could have been forgiven for thinking they could sell anything on wheels; but come sales time they were struggling. No future historian, however, would detect any sign of austerity by looking at the cars rather than at their sales figures; the luxury market always survives.

The 1957 Lincolns were based on the extremely well-received 1956 cars, which had actually been on the drawing board since 1953. Until 1955 Lincoln's latest theme had been luxury coupled with performance in a reasonably compact car, such as the 'Road Race' Capri. When the dramatically different new series was unveiled for 1956, size was added to luxury and power and given glamorous new packaging. Capri was moved from top to bottom series and the new Premiere became the flagship. All the new Lincolns were substantially bigger and sleeker. Wheelbase went up to 126in, overall length grew by some seven inches and width by three inches, but the cars were slightly lower, very little heavier and there was a powerful new 368cu in V8. Tom McCahill in *Mechanix Illustrated* enthused: 'For 1956, Lincoln has done the impossible: they've built safety and roadability into a huge car. Here is a heavyweight with all the agility and flashy reflexes of the fastest featherweight'.

If anything, the 1957 cars were even an improvement on the 1956s, and Lincoln introduced a completely new body style to their line for the first time in several years: the four-door hardtop Premiere Landau. Sales for 1956 had been good, at almost 50,000 units, but with a four-door hardtop in the line then they might have been even better. The Landau was just a little too late.

The 1956 Premiere Coupé had won the Industrial Designers Institution Award for its styling and the 1957 stayed much the same shape, although unfortunately it did not escape entirely the blight of added gimmicks. The overall impression was still of speed and power, which was probably the right image to promote at a time when the government was pushing ahead with its $33 billion programme for an interstate 'superhighway' system. The 1957 Premiere retained the massive, horizontal chrome grille theme, but the fairly understated chrome side spears of 1956 gave way to a more elaborate side treatment with a full-length chrome styling line and a chrome-plated slash strip in the top half of the rear door, marking the leading edge of much enlarged fins. The biggest difference of all was the first appearance of 'Quadri-Lites', a two-up, two-down arrangement which was actually two headlights and two fog lights rather than four headlights.

For all that, the Premiere was restrained by 1957 standards. It offered eighteen body colours, almost eighty two-tone combinations and over forty interior trim packages. A new idea in the interior was horizontal pleating in the seats, and the range of quality leather and cloth materials was typical of Lincoln.

Safety was being plugged by most Ford products of the time, and the Lincoln was no exception. At last, Lincoln offered a properly padded dash, the centre of the steering wheel was deeply recessed to accommodate a 3½-inch thick energy absorbing cushion, and impact-resistant locks (pioneered by Chrysler almost twenty years earlier) were standard. Seat-belts were offered as an option but were only specified by about one buyer in ten.

As well as the safety options, the Premiere had plenty of creature comforts. Power brakes, steering, seats and windows were standard, as was normal for a car in this league, and the latest, improved air-conditioning option could give a complete air change in one minute. Even the vent windows were powered, and there were such options as remote-control outside mirrors, self-seeking radio and automatic headlight dimming.

Mechanically, the car was a worthy successor to the sporty Capris. The Premiere had slightly softer suspension than its predecessor, to provide a slightly softer ride, but in spite of a little more body roll it remained stable and sure-footed. For anyone who understood such refinements at the time, the Premiere also offered a limited slip differential, going by the name 'Directed Power', and 'Adjust-O-Matic' adjustable shock absorbers. As the latter, in spite of the name, were adjustable only at the wheel (road, not steering) their appeal to the typical Lincoln owner is doubtful. Performance was very high on the list of desirable features for any mid-1950s American auto, but straight-line, drag strip performance, not round-the-bend race track performance.

For 1957 the 368 V8 was improved by virtue of reshaped pistons and combustion chambers and improved carburation (among other things) to give a very useful 300hp and an enormous 415lb ft of torque, at a relatively high 3000rpm. This gave the Premiere performance in the order of 105mph top speed and eleven-second 0–60mph times, with quite reasonable fuel economy.

Although the product was excellent (rated as such by eighty-five per cent of owners in an independent survey and criticized only occasionally for poor detail assembly, causing body rattles) Lincoln were outsold in the luxury market, for the first and only time, by Imperial. Like many another good car before and since, the 1957 Lincoln was a one-year wonder. In 1958 it was replaced by another, longer, lower and wider Lincoln, possibly one of the worst cars of all time.

SPECIFICATION	
Model 1957 Lincoln Premiere	
Engine type ohv V8	
Bore × stroke 4.0 × 3.66in	
Capacity 368cu in	
Compression ratio 10.0:1	
Carburation 1 × 4bbl	
Max. power 300hp @ 4800rpm	
Transmission Turbo-Drive	
Wheelbase 126in	
Weight 4527lb	
Price $5294	

Pages 96–7 and left: the 1957 Premiere came in a wide range of body styles and was available in a vast array of paint and trim combinations. It was widely acknowledged to be a good car, even by Lincoln standards, but in 1957, for the one and only time, Lincoln was outsold by the upstart Imperial

THE ROMANS' MYTHOLOGICAL winged messenger of the gods never sprouted wings quite so elaborate as those of his latter-day namesake from Ford, but then he only had to cruise the heavens, not the turnpike, and not in 1957. That year's Mercury Turnpike Cruiser would probably have looked somewhat out of place in ancient Rome, too; it was even a little uncomfortable on home ground.

Subtlety was not a recurring styling theme in 1957, but it took most manufacturers until 1958 really to abandon all restraint and hit the highways with their grossest excesses. Mercury was ahead of everyone else with the 1957 Turnpike Cruiser; there was almost nothing about it that would not eventually appear again elsewhere and be a sell-out, but, instead of introducing their ideas a bit at a time, Mercury put virtually all their novelties into one package which proved to be too much for the public, too soon. This is not to say that the Turnpike Cruiser was a bad car, but, much like its famous cousin the Edsel, it was misjudged and mistimed.

It started life in 1956 as one of the stars of Ford's motor shows – their own slightly less grand equivalent of General Motors' elaborate and influential Motoramas. It was then called the Mercury XM Turnpike Cruiser and as such it became a famous sight on the road, as well as in the exhibition halls, towed from one show to another, nationwide, in a specially built, glass-sided trailer. The sales pitch went that the XM was designed 'to give American motorists maximum driving pleasure, comfort and safety as they travel the new turnpikes' and its exceptionally large glass area was said to be there 'to permit full enjoyment of the wide new vistas opened to turnpike travellers'. Such claims were, of course, a supreme piece of marketing optimism, cashing in on the passing of the Interstate Highway Act of 1956, which promised a vast and much-needed expansion of the freeway system over the coming years.

The 1957 production version of the Turnpike Cruiser was somewhat toned down from the show car, but was unmistakably closely related. It had a simpler roofline (which was not difficult), more conventional, if still very gaudy, grille and bumpers, and far less extreme versions of the huge double tail fins of the original. On the other hand, its menacingly hooded twin headlights, jutting forward on extraordinary ribbed chrome barrels, were even more garish than the single lights of the XM. It was the top Mercury model for 1957 and available as two- and four-door hardtops and a convertible. The convertible was a replica of the one used as the Pace Car for the Indy 500, but it was not a big seller.

Apart from the radical styling, several of the better features of the show car found their way onto the production model. The Turnpike Cruiser had a flattened top to the steering wheel, to allow a clear view of the instruments (and, presumably, the 'wide new vistas' beyond). The instruments included an average-speed computer, then an innovation, in a comprehensive package. The Cruiser also boasted a forty-nine-position 'memory seat' with the unimaginative name of 'Seat-O-Matic'. The reverse-sloping rear window was retractable and there were dual fresh-air vents along the top edge of the compound-curve, wraparound windshield. One problem that the auto engineers never did quite overcome was how to make a windshield-wiper that would clean round corners, but then it never seemed to be raining in the *Saturday Evening Post* ads.

The power train for the 1957 Turnpike Cruiser comprised the 'small block' derivative, 368cu in V8, delivering a respectable 290hp through a two-speed Merc-O-Matic transmission, which pre-dated the Edsel in using push-button selection. Power brakes and power steering were standard equipment on the Turnpike Cruiser, which weighed just over 4000lb. In spite of its size, the Cruiser was brutally quick off the line – over 400lb ft of torque saw to that – and it had a top speed approaching 110mph, not quite as quick as the winged messenger, perhaps, but respectable.

The price for all this refinement and novelty was the price; had the Turnpike Cruiser been considerably cheaper than it was, had it been a bit less outrageously styled, and had the romance of turnpike cruising existed more as it had in the advertising imagery, the car might have caught on. As things were, only 16,861 copies, including 1265 convertibles (which represented an allocation of one to each dealer) were sold in 1957.

For 1958, the Cruiser became just a variant of the Montclair and it ran head on into the competition of its sister, Edsel. At the end of the 1958 model year it was dropped, never to be seen again. Maybe the gods had preferred the original.

SPECIFICATION

Model 1957 Mercury
 Turnpike Cruiser

Engine type ohv V8
Bore × stroke 4.0 × 3.66in
Capacity 368cu in
Compression ratio 10.0:1
Carburation 1 × 4bbl
Max. power 290hp
 @ 4600rpm

Transmission Merc-O-Matic

Wheelbase 122in
Weight 4240lb

Price $4103

Pages 100–101 and left: all dressed up and nowhere to go. The convertible version of the Turnpike Cruiser was a spectacular sight, as would be any car so closely based on a show offering. It was by no means a bad car, but there were cheaper ways to see the wide vistas promised in the advertising copy, and the Big M lost out to most of them

IN 1957 PLYMOUTH PROCLAIMED 'Suddenly it's 1960'. The time machine which allegedly rocketed the auto into the future was the new 1957 Plymouth range, styled by Virgil Exner and as good looking a creation as you could wish to see.

Building on the success of his dramatic restyling for 1955 (which coincided with the introduction of V8 power), Exner was rapidly dragging Plymouth out of the troubles that dogged them through the first half of the 1950s. Until 1955 Plymouth, the low-cost member of the Chrysler Corporation line-up, stood for cheap, economical, no-frills, no-thrills autos. They were solid, well built and reliable, but they were dull; doyen of auto writers Tom McCahill once opined that Plymouth was a good name for a rock. Exner's styling and the engineering department's discovery of horsepower (a discovery shared with the rest of Chrysler) changed all that and transformed Plymouths into some of the best cars in the business.

The year 1957 was probably the most stylish of all for the division, a step or two ahead of the already handsome 1956 cars, which introduced the Forward Look, and a merciful step short of what would evolve for 1959, when fins and flashiness dominated the entire industry. Plymouth's high card was once again the sporting Fury, an evocative name for a thrill-a-minute car. When Chrysler had started to cultivate the sporting image after the introduction of their 'modern' overhead-valve V8, each division was given its own performance machine of the day. The first Fury, a white convertible with an anodized gold stripe on its flank, was a mid-season 1956 introduction, with a 240hp, 303cu in V8. Mid-season introductions of muscle cars were a ploy to satisfy the rule requiring 90-days' notice of a new model before eligibility for the ever-more important NASCAR stock racing circuit, and at the time Chrysler were masters of the art. In fact, the Fury was never any great success on the racing circuit, but more than made up for this in the market-place.

In 1957 the Fury grew up. It rode on a 118-inch wheelbase, three inches longer than before, it looked altogether bigger and sleeker and it was given even more power. Plymouths now had some of the biggest fins in the industry, certainly the biggest in their price range. They were also some of the most finely styled. The Fury now came as a supremely elegant hardtop coupé which had the most glass, the lowest waistline and some of the cleanest looks of the year, the hardtop roofline in particular being quite extraordinarily graceful and simple. There was no unnecessary ornament; the grille was uncluttered and tasteful and the only side decoration was a slim, contrasting spear. Inside, the car was as elegant as it was outside, with cloth and vinyl trim and a straightforward, easy-to-read dashboard set

just where it should be, directly ahead of the driver. All in all, the Fury could hardly have looked better.

With all this and more power, a new transmission and much improved suspension it is not surprising that the 1957 Fury has a reputation as one of the best Plymouths ever. Its new engine was up in capacity to 318cu in and horsepower was now a sabre-rattling 290, more than either Ford or Chevrolet. Plymouth's new V8s were extremely popular and the marque sold a far higher proportion of V8s to sixes than even Chevrolet, whose superb V8 had also been introduced in 1955. Plymouth also had a sudden upsurge in the popularity of its automatic transmission options, again to lead both Ford and Chevrolet, since it introduced push-button control in 1956. For 1957 there was a new automatic for cars like the Fury: the Torque-Flite. As if this were not enough for a car in Plymouth's price range to offer, 1957 also marked the introduction of torsion-bar front suspension

to the range, another first for a car in this class, even though it had been acclaimed on far more expensive offerings. Torsion bars and further improved rear-suspension geometry made the 1957 Plymouths the smoothest-riding and best-handling examples of the marque to date.

In just about every way, the Fury and its ilk were a triumph and, for once, their excellence was not wasted on a fickle market-place. Plymouth sales took off again in 1957 and, when the receipts were totted up at the end of the year, the division had sold 655,526 cars, including the ten-millionth Plymouth, built in January. With a forty-five per cent sales increase over the previous year the result was good enough to edge Plymouth ahead of Buick again into third place in the industry sales league. That was one of the most fitting tributes of all to a car which today ranks high among the classics of the decade.

SPECIFICATION

Model 1957 Plymouth Fury

Engine type ohv V8
Bore × stroke 3.906 ×
   3.312in
Capacity 318cu in
Compression ratio 9.25:1
Carburation 2 × 4bbl
Max. power 290hp
   @ 5400rpm

Transmission Torque-Flite

Wheelbase 118in
Weight 3595lb

Price $2925

Pages 104–5: this 1957 Fury is housed in the Yesterday Once More collection of musician Richard Carpenter. The Fury nameplate and the evocative shape are perfect partners in the Chrysler performance family

Left: push-button control for the excellent Torque-Flite transmission put Plymouth in the forefront of automatic sales, and the stylish interiors helped too

Right: side-by-side head and park lamps gave a dual headlight look

'THE MOST REFRESHING, stimulating and progressively styled car to emerge from a stock car manufacturer since the days of the Lincoln Continental and the coffin-nosed Cord.' Thus did *Motor Trend* magazine describe the newly unveiled 1953 Studebaker Starliner, and they were right. It was one of a new range of Studebakers which celebrated a hundred years as a vehicle builder for Studebaker, who had started by building horse-drawn carriages. These latest cars were stunningly different from anything else America had to offer. The basic shape of that 1953 classic would carry Studebaker to the end of a commercially shaky decade and would grace one of the most spectacular of the many spectacular American cars of the 1950s, the Studebaker Golden Hawk.

The Golden Hawk was a short-lived bird, lasting only from 1956 to 1958, and model year 1957 represented the peak of the car's brief ascendancy. As always in the fickle American auto market, style and innovation were not enough, and Studebaker was soon to follow the Hawks into extinction.

What the customers were not buying was a car little short of sensational in looks and engineering. The Golden Hawk was introduced, as top of a range of Hawks, in 1956. It was a five-seat, two-door hardtop descended from the beautiful Virgil Exner/Raymond Loewy-styled Starliner, with low sweeping lines of pure, uncluttered simplicity. The overall appearance would suffer a little in succeeding years from the blight of gilding the lily with decoration for decoration's sake, but that was largely forced upon Studebaker by the need to show something new without being able to afford it. The 1957 Golden Hawk's cosmetic package stopped a step short of the gaudy pinnacles of 1958. Its fins were only large, not absurdly so, and although they were trimmed with golden appliqué, the overall look was still quite clean. Mechanically, moreover, the 1957 car was a giant step ahead of its predecessor.

Studebaker pushed the Golden Hawk as 'America's First Family-Size Sports Car' and advertised 'All the Fun of Sports Car Performance'. These were only mild overstatements. The 1956 car had used the 352cu in Packard V8, whose 275hp and massive 380lb ft of torque meant vivid performance. The main drawback with the big motor in the 120½ inch-wheelbase car was simply that all that weight up front made the Hawk difficult in corners – although by 1956 standards it was less difficult than most. What made the 1957 Golden Hawk so much more civilized was a new engine – a supercharged version of the long-stroke 289cu in Studebaker V8. While this engine did not have quite the torque of the big Packard, it did have exactly the same horsepower and it offered a worthwhile weight saving.

This combination did little to harm the Golden

Hawk's straight-line performance, and by virtue of improved (though still nose-heavy) front-to-rear weight distribution it imparted a new precision to the handling. It was still not sports car handling in the European idiom of course, but to America it was 'Gran Turismo'. The Golden Hawk with a three-speed, overdrive, manual transmission and low axle ratio was tested at just under 7½ seconds to run 0–60mph, which was not as fast as the contemporaneous Corvette but was a good second faster than Ford's Thunderbird. What's more, at just over 127mph the Golden Hawk was fastest overall of that sporting trio.

The 'Gran Turismo' epithet was not entirely wishful

thinking; the Golden Hawk actually could pass as a comfortable, high-speed tourer for four or, at a pinch, five passengers, with the sort of appointments more usual on European cars. For example, the dashboard was remarkably informative for an American car of the period. In addition to a speedometer which read, a trifle fancifully, to 160mph, it had a tachometer and a vacuum gauge, and the switches were of simple and efficient toggle type. Performance was not achieved through brute force and ignorance; the Paxton centrifugal supercharger was driven through a variable rate pulley which allowed it to produce maximum effect when the accelerator was pressed hard but which would operate

SPECIFICATION

Model 1957 Golden Hawk

Engine type ohv V8
Bore × stroke 3.562 × 3.625in
Capacity 289.1cu in
Compression ratio 7.8:1
Carburation 1 × 4bbl s'chgd
Max. power 275hp @ 4800rpm

Wheelbase 120.5in
Weight 3400lb

Price $3182

Below: the Hawks of the late 1950s were direct descendants of the Raymond Loewy/Virgil Exner designs launched in 1953, and regarded as some of the best looking of all American autos. Even so, Studebaker was doomed

Following page, top left: the lighter, supercharged engine transformed Golden Hawk handling in 1957

virtually at a freewheel when the car was cruising, without the demand for extra power. This gave the Studebaker the almost unique distinction of combining performance with acceptable fuel economy.

Sadly, Studebaker had long suffered from the fact that they could not complement their imaginative engineering projects with the bread-and-butter cars which would give them essential strength in the mass market. Since their merger with the struggling Packard company in 1954, Studebaker had existed almost from day to day, in spite of a later management agreement with the powerful Curtiss-Wright corporation. The Golden Hawk was modified again for 1958, following the all-too-obvious route of bigger fins and more trim, although it did benefit from further suspension

improvement. Through the Hawk series of 1957, sales had shown some signs of an upturn and even the exotic Golden Hawk sold an encouraging 4536 units, but it was really only buying time. By 1958 the Packard name was no more and the aggressive Hawk gave way to the meeker, more compact Lark, at least in the sales race. While the Hawk name continued until 1964 on Canadian-built Studebakers and its engineering novelty survived right to the bitter end in 1966, the Golden Hawk flew no more after 1958.

Motor Trend should probably be allowed the last word of this sad tale, as well as the first. Its description of the Starliner had gone on to say 'it may also be too far advanced in styling concept for the public to accept'. Once again, they were right.

IT WAS ALL change at Buick in 1958; management came and went and the 1958 Buicks were one of a kind, a massive overreaction to the division's disastrous fall-off in sales from the heady peaks of 1955. Subtle they were not but, as an illustration of the heights (or depths) which the chrome age reached, they have few peers. In a year they were gone, but never forgotten.

In 1955, the industry's best-ever year, Buick had had record sales of almost 750,000 cars, held on to third place in the market and sold the millionth Riviera. Buick's reputation for quality was slipping, however. Quality control sometimes took second place to production needs. The slogan 'when better automobiles are built, Buick will build them' did not quite hold true at the time. In 1956 sales slipped and in 1957 they slumped. Something drastic was needed for 1958 and the Century Riviera was certainly that.

The 1957 cars had been completely restyled at enormous expense. They were longer and lower and the stylists were adding more glitter to the trim. The 1957 Buicks sported a new roofline which forsook the simple sweeps of before for over-fussy new shapes. On some cars two chrome strips ran over the roofline, down the rear window and on towards the rear of the car. Offered a choice of this style or the simpler, earlier look, buyers took the uncluttered option; given the choice between a Buick and the new, tail-finned, 'Forward Look' Plymouths (styled by Chrysler's Virgil Exner), buyers took the Plymouth, and Plymouth took third place in the sales race.

The 1958 Buicks were Harley Earl's hastily conceived counter-attack, and they were monstrous. The 1958 Century Riviera is typical. Gone were the relatively lithe lines of the earlier cars, and in their place came Earl's 'heavy look' in which weight was equated with wealth: a bigger-looking Buick was meant to suggest some financial substance in its owner. The 1958 body panels were rounded out and chrome was ladled on wherever it would hang. It probably seemed like a good idea at the time. Over the top of a huge bumper, with ship's prow overriders, was a grille of surpassing vulgarity, comprising 160 chrome-plated, light-reflecting, four-faceted, die-cast squares, topped off by a huge top lip and flanked by ornate, bullet-shaped, chromed sidelight clusters. This whole dazzling confection extended all the way round to the leading edges of the front wheel arches and it had a name: the 'Fashion-Aire Dynastar Grille'. As a joke in poor taste, it went well with the Vista Vision twin headlights, topped with chromed 'gunsights' on each front fender. The rear end was even more massively overstated, but who cared? The Sweepspear was supplemented by a chrome and brushed-aluminium motif which looked faster than a speeding bullet. The Century Riviera, alas, was not.

SPECIFICATION

Model 1958 Buick Century
Riviera

Engine type ohv V8
Bore × stroke 4.125 × 3.4in
Capacity 364cu in
Compression ratio 10.0:1
Carburation 1 × 4bbl
Max. power 300hp
@ 4600rpm

Transmission Dynaflow

Wheelbase 122in
Weight 4267lb

Price $3119

Preceding page, left and below left:
the two-door Century Riviera
was probably the best of a rather
embarrassing 1958 crop for
Buick. Its bulbous fender lines
and the amazing amount of
chrome are typical of the time
when weight meant wealth to the
GM stylists, but disastrous sales
results brought anything but
wealth to the beleaguered Buick
division. The Century's rear trim
panels were styled in the usual
rocket image but could more
easily be mistaken for chrome-
plated grave digging shovels,
which Buick came periously close
to needing

Right: Fashion–Aire Dynaster
grille, Vista–Vision twin headlights and chromed 'gunsights'
heralded the Century's arrival
and speeded its departure

The V8 had grown to 364cu in and power options ranged from 250–300hp but, with an extra 400 pounds of strictly non-functional hardware to haul around, the 1958 Century was nowhere near as sharp as its road-burning brothers of yore, when the Century was simply the lightest body with the strongest motor. The 1955 Century, for example, with 236hp and a Variable Pitch Dynaflow, could reach 60mph in under ten seconds, and every 1956 Buick could better 100mph. The Air-Born B-58 Buick (as it was unfortunately dubbed by the ad-men) had as an option what was in theory the industry's most technically advanced auto, the triple-turbine Flight-Pitch Dynaflow, but this unit, which offered hydraulic torque multiplication throughout the speed range, was problematic, difficult to manufacture, inefficient, and lacked any feel of control – even though the figures suggested that it was delivering the goods. Its development cost over $85 million of corporate funds, and when Buick's market share fell from around 5.7 per cent to just over 4 per cent in 1958 there were a few who feared for the division's future.

As an option, the 1958 Buick could be quite literally air-borne, with Air-Poise air suspension on all four corners as an alternative to the usual coil springs. Sadly, Air-Poise too was a near-disaster. The pressurized cylinder assemblies, on which the self-levelling, self-jacking system relied for springing, had a tendency to leak and bring the car to its knees. When it *was* working correctly, Air-Poise was soft and bouncy and there were always problems with the suspension bottoming out over bumps. In 1959, Air-Poise was confined to rear-only options and a year later it had disappeared altogether.

Perhaps the one saving grace for the 1958 Buicks was their new brakes. After years of problems with inconsistent drums, premature fade and even total failure, Buick engineers finally came up with the best brakes in the industry. By the relatively simple expedient of grafting a finned aluminium cooling cover on to the front cast-iron drums, Buick made a composite brake that, for stopping power and fade resistance, was second to none.

The brakes, but little else, would be carried over to the completely new 1959 line. Even the tarnished names would be changed. The amazing decorative excesses of 1958 (which had even extended to a ludicrous, heavily sculpted, chrome and brushed-aluminium dash, which copied the outside rocket motif) marked the pinnacle of an era. Buick had finally gone clean over the top and given the public just too much of what had once been a good thing. Now sanity could return. The 1958 Buicks were certainly memorable autos, but they were not the ones by which Buick would have liked to be remembered.

CHEVROLET ADVERTISING CALLED the 1958 Impala 'The most daringly conceived car ever introduced in the low-price field! And the most glamorous Chevrolet you ever laid eyes on ... incredibly lower, excitingly longer, and loaded with touches exclusively its own. Its Sculpturamic beauty hails a new styling era – a new pinnacle of prestige!' Give or take a superlative or two, the description was not too wide of the mark; the Impala was another General Motors style-leader.

GM's Golden Anniversary was in 1958, and the theme for the year was 'Forward from Fifty'. The new Chevys were certainly a step in that direction in terms of looks. They were up to seven inches longer than the 1957s and they were lower, wider and substantially heavier. A new name on a new series, Impala had first been used on a Motorama car shown in 1956, and the 1958 Impala was a sub-series of the popular Bel Air, available only as a sport coupé or a convertible. It had a lot to live up to: since the arrival of Ed Cole's brilliant, compact V8 for 1955, Chevys had been fine driver's cars.

The Impala, however, was a far cry from the quick, sporting, sharp handling Chevrolets which had proved their worth in NASCAR racing and at Daytona, where the quickest 1957 car had topped 131mph. There would be none of this in 1958, though, because during 1957 the Automobile Manufacturers Association, worried by an ever-increasing emphasis on performance, had banned direct factory involvement in racing. This didn't put a stop to the Chevrolet engine's winning ways with 'private' teams, but it did put an end to advertising themes such as 'The Hot One's Even Hotter' and 'Chevy Comes to the Line *Loaded* for '57!' With racing suddenly discredited, the new Impala was not aimed at the performance freak but at a completely new market sector for Chevrolet – the more staid, more substantial, Pontiac price-range buyer, who wanted a big, comfortable car. This was exactly what Chevrolet now offered them.

The 1958 Impala was on the longest wheelbase, 117½ inches, of any Chevrolet since 1919. At only $2841 the Impala Convertible was the year's most expensive Chevy but still the industry's cheapest soft top. For a low-priced car its engineering was impressive. Its X-frame was a third stronger than the previous year's and the Fisher bodies were rigid and rattle resistant, thanks to massive side rails, a double-skinned, full-width cowl and solid cross-members joining body to frame. To a degree it made up for more weight with more cubic inches, and the top option was a big new 250hp, 348cu in V8, coupled to the excellent Turbo Hydra-Matic transmission, but show was more important than 'go' and ride was more important than handling. Gone were the boasts of race car roadholding; the 1958 Impala promised 'the road smoothingest, nerve soothingest

ride imaginable ... on a new Full Coil Suspension that glides you through a "calm sea" of road'. In other words, on its low-pressure tubeless tyres, the Impala rode like a boat. The only real concession to sporty performance was improved Anti-Dive braking, although the brakes were barely good enough to promote much dive in the first place.

The Impala's size was cleverly emphasized by its styling, which was altogether rounder and heavier than before. This was pretty much an industry trend, meant to imply substance, and rather embarrassing as the 1958 recession began to bite. Chevy, however, rebelled against the obsession of the day – bigger and bigger fins. Ford and Chrysler had had restylings for 1957 while Chevrolet had only a face-lift, but now it was GM's turn. 'Sculpturamic' was what Chevrolet called their new look, and that meant long, low and heavily sculpted sides and restrained, almost elegant, fins that curved outwards along the car and swept back round the surprisingly neat cluster of three tail lights on each side. The fins were simply trimmed with fine chrome edging, but the clean effect was spoiled by an excess of chrome and polished aluminium trim virtually everywhere else.

Still, it made the other manufacturers sit up and look at their own gaudy efforts and worry at the way Chevrolet's first quad headlight set-up was an obvious pointer to a new, up-market challenge.

Being a Chevy, the Impala was basically a low-priced car which could be topped up with virtually any option the salesman could think of, including power brakes and steering, power seats and windows, tinted glass, heater, radio, air conditioning and even a Vacuum Ash Tray which sucked cigarettes to oblivion at a touch.

Chevrolet sold 60,000 Impalas from a total of around 1¼ million sales, enough to regain the number one market slot from Ford but poor by Chevrolet standards. Buyers were happy, it seems, with a floating ride, vague steering and marginal brakes as long as they were offset by a roomy and well-trimmed interior and a suggestion of affluence. Nevertheless, Sculpturamic styling lasted only a year before a complete rethink brought the infamous gull-wing Impala shape. The 1958 Impala was one in a row, neither as sharp as its predecessors nor as overblown as its followers, but with an appeal all its own. Fortunately, as comparisons are odious, it can be remembered for what it is.

Pages 116–7 and right: the full, rounded look of the 1958 Impala was what Chevrolet hailed as 'Sculpturamic beauty'. It was another one-year wonder, replaced by the distinctive gull-wing look as part of GM's 'planned obsolescence' and inner-body sharing programme. This was probably the closest GM came to aesthetic success with the bulbous look

Left: the neat air-extractor vent at the trailing edge of the roof

SINCE 1948 THE DESIGNATION 'E-car' within Ford had meant 'experimental car'. Come E-day, 4 September 1957, it meant Edsel. It was not revolutionary, it was just different enough. In the year when styling excesses went through the roof, it might even have been considered conservative. True, the horse-collar grille was rather startling, but then in 1958 there were few real shocks left to deliver in auto styling. The biggest shock of all was to come when Ford read the sales reports.

Although never intended to be the new car's name, Edsel became one of the most famous names in automobile history, the butt of jokes and symbol of failure. Yet the Edsel was not a bad car – it was just that its timing was all wrong. If any car in history should have succeeded the Edsel was it. Ford knew that they needed a car between the Ford and Mercury ranges;

three out of four Ford buyers were simply not moving up to Mercury the way that Chevrolet buyers were moving up to Pontiac, Buick and Oldsmobile, or Plymouth buyers to Dodge and Chrysler. So, Ford undertook what was then the most extensive and costly market-research programme ever mounted, to discover exactly what the new car should offer, and then they ploughed some $250 million into turning that car into reality. They even asked the public for a name, but they didn't get one they liked. So Edsel it was, after Henry's son and Henry II's father.

When the Edsel division was created, in 1955, the industry and the market were booming. Nothing could have been more natural than to plan a big, powerful, highly styled car for three years ahead; everyone else was. By the time Edsel was built, however, things had

changed dramatically. September 1957 not only saw the launch of the Edsel, but also the start of the worst three months of that year's recession. The Edsel never stood a chance.

The Citation was the top of the four-line 1958 range, alongside the Corsair and the more basic Ranger and Pacer. It was everything it was designed to be, but there was no longer a demand for it. It was a big car, over 18 feet long on a 124-inch wheelbase, and it used a 410cu in V8, whose massive 345hp punch and 475lb ft of torque made the upper-range Edsel a very quick car indeed of its kind. A Citation could reach 60mph in around 9½ seconds, and such power (derived from the even larger, 430cu in Lincoln engine), which made the Citation a quiet and effortless performer, was far from wasted in the well-designed and well-engineered Edsel package.

SPECIFICATION

Model 1958 Edsel Citation

Engine type ohv V8
Bore × stroke 4.2 × 3.7in
Capacity 410cu in
Compression ratio 10.5:1
Carburation 1 × 4bbl
Max. power 345hp
 @ 4600rpm

Transmission Teletouch

Wheelbase 124in
Weight 4230lb

Price $3615

Above: there but for the grace of God goes almost every car ever made

Following page: steering wheel auto push buttons and novel dash layout were among Edsel innovations

Page 123: 'like an Oldsmobile sucking a lemon'. Had names commissioned from the poet Marianne Moore been adopted, the badge might have read 'Mongoose Civique' or 'Utopian Turtletop'

The Citation's standard equipment automatic transmission was controlled by 'Teletouch Drive', with push-buttons in the centre of the steering wheel. The system was a novelty, certainly, but not just a gimmick – it was both functional and reliable. A generously proportioned, revolving-drum speedometer, on a binnacle dash which also housed a tachometer, was another novelty, while a warning light on the dash could be set to flash to the driver at a predetermined speed, not a bad idea with 345hp on tap.

Although a quick car in a straight line, the Citation earned few plaudits for its roadholding and handling, which were the object of much criticism. Largely because of its size and power, there was a necessary compromise of light steering and soft ride, although the self-adjusting drum brakes were not bad. Not surprisingly, with such a huge motor, it had a powerful thirst and the 1958 models also suffered somewhat from the malady of the times, poor quality control. That aside, the few Edsels that were sold just kept running.

The early production goal was around 300,000 Edsels a year, but less than 55,000 saw the light of day in 1957. That paltry number plummeted to a disastrous 27,000-odd in 1958, and up to 19 November 1959 only another 30,000 or so were made. By then Ford had tried most possibilities with the Edsel, including complete restyling, which made the car little more than a badge-engineered Ford, and the option of far more frugal powerplants than the big Lincoln derivative. Within weeks of the 4 September launch, sales had fallen to half the level needed to break even and there were immediate breaks in the ranks of the 1150 or so top-line dealers, many of whom Ford had stolen from Chrysler and GM. Within a few years, Ford would virtually deny that the Edsel ever existed, but twenty years later the most famous flop of all was to find a steady cult following and more market interest than it ever had in its day.

Ford closed down the Edsel division after 2846 of the much more conventional 1960 models had been built. In retrospect they might have tried harder. The faults were really trifling and the Edsel deserved to succeed. The reason it did not was simply that it ran into the 1958 market's rediscovered resistance to novelty. Had the Edsel happened six months earlier or six months later, it might have been a very different story.

LINCOLN AND CONTINENTAL are often confused, largely because Continental existed as a separate marque from 1956 to 1960 and Lincoln used Continental as a model name during the same period. This 1958 Lincoln Continental Mark III was a true Lincoln, unlike the 1956 Continental Mark II, which was a Continental. The 1968 Continental Mark III (not to be confused with this 1958 *Lincoln* Continental Mark III) would also be a Continental in name, rather than a Lincoln. Anything else built after 1961 which bore the name Continental, be it Lincoln Continental or Continental Mark whatever, was a Lincoln from the Lincoln division.

There might have been a true Continental Mark III for 1958, but designs by John Reinhardt (who styled the classic Mark II) were rejected and the Lincoln Continental Mark III was hurriedly created to capitalize on the magical name. It shared the same basic shell as the Capri and Premiere, but was subtly different and unmistakably superior.

Ford's 1955 brief for the new 1958 Lincolns was to outrank Cadillac in every area: size, space, power and style. Size, space and power were entrusted to engineering, under Harley Copp (who engineered the Mark II and soon wished he had never heard of the Mark III), and John Najjar was appointed by George Walker as chief stylist.

In spite of strenuous protests from Copp, engineering boss Earle McPherson decreed that the Mark III would have a unit construction body, partly (and in theory) to give a better ratio of interior space to exterior dimensions but mostly to take up surplus production capacity alongside the flagging Thunderbird. Copp's misgivings were about the car's size; unit construction had so far been used mostly on fairly small (and usually European) autos and its advantages were known to diminish with size. Nobody really knew the critical point, but Copp thought that the Lincoln was beyond it. His problem was compounded by his only having two years to make the car work and when the first prototype was finished, in May 1956, his fears proved all too well founded. The 131-inch wheelbase body shell, destined to be the largest six-passenger car on the 1958 market, had about as much torsional stiffness as a piece of string; the rear quarter of one prototype collapsed under bump testing. The palliative was grafted-on stiffening, which meant more weight and prompted an engine even bigger than originally envisaged – up to a monstrous 430cu in. This added up to a car weighing 5000lb or more, which caused problems with the rear coil springs going their own way over a really severe bump, and kept plans for an air-suspension system unfulfilled. It is a huge tribute to Copp's team that, in the end, the car was no worse than it was.

By comparison, Najjar's problems were trifling. He

SPECIFICATION

Model 1958 Lincoln
  Continental Mark III

Engine type ohv V8
Bore × stroke 4.3 × 3.7in
Capacity 430cu in
Compression ratio 10.5:1
Carburation 1 × 4bbl
Max. power 375hp
  @ 4800rpm

Transmission Multi-Drive

Wheelbase 131in
Weight 5040lb

Price $6283

Preceding page: combining a Ford corporate look with a shape radically different from those of the opposition was no easy task by the late 1950s, when almost every stylistic trick had already been tried, but the Lincoln Continental Mark III was somehow given a very strong identity

Left: the power-operated soft-top was a much less horrific engineering problem than the contemporary Ford's retractable hardtop

Right: 'continental' wheel mount and 'a grille at each end'

had to produce a car that was totally individual, 'tasteful, smart and with dignity'. Huge fins were out because they were Cadillac's domain, and the wedge look spelt Imperial, so that was another non-starter. Najjar eventually hit on a rectangular look, of the Ford type but distinctive. Dual headlights canted out at the front and the small fins and lamps at the rear followed them. The base of the car flared outward, heavily emphasized by the massive bumper tips. There was very little chrome on the flanks but there was a distinctive scalloped front fender design which mimicked a long wheel-arch cut-out. The rear window was the big trick item; where other Lincolns had wraparound glass, the Continental had a reverse sloping panel which power-retracted into the trunk at the touch of a button, giving very effective ventilation as well as a 'look'. Taking earlier Lincoln themes to a logical conclusion, the Mark III had a 'grille' at each end. The interiors, perversely for such a massive car, were no bigger than the 1957 cars, but they were traditionally Lincoln in finish, with typically sumptuous Lincoln appointments.

Lincoln certainly succeeded in their avowed intent of being bigger and more powerful than Cadillac, in every dimension and with 375 standard or 400 optional horsepower compared to a mere 310. Such horsepower and a staggering 490lb ft of torque gave 0–60 acceleration times around the nine-second mark, exceptionally quick for a 5000lb auto. Today it might be considered gross and wallowing, but at the time the Mark III was hailed as 'amazingly nimble'. Even with almost forty-five per cent more brake area, the brakes were guaranteed to fade after four or five stops from even 60mph and a couple of shakes later they would disappear altogether; it was that sort of car.

Although the Lincoln was the only all-new offering from the luxury marques in 1958, and although it was by far the biggest and most powerful, it was an abject failure in sales terms. The Continental outsold the cheaper Capris and Premieres, but Lincoln were last but one in the whole industry. The cars were much criticized by owners, initially because the unit bodies rattled, then, after tolerances had been tightened, because the fit was so close that the doors jammed. For 1959, this magnificent aberration was softened slightly in terms of styling and tightened in terms of construction, but the damage was already done and its days were numbered.

PROBABLY THE BEST thing that can be said about 1958, as far as Oldsmobile styling goes, is that General Motors made 1958 the first year of its 'planned obsolescence' programme. Over the years, the planned lifespan of each new model had become generally shorter and shorter. After a decent period to recover and capitalize on expensive tooling costs, a complete restyling or major mechanical rehash was made and, lo and behold, the customer had to buy the new model or become a social leper. That, at least, was the theory and, by and large, it worked. In 1958 GM set out to take it to its logical conclusion. By completely redesigning its ranges each season (but saving some costs by introducing more sharing of inner body panels between divisions) it would encourage the astute buyer to trade in his car every year, hence 'planned obsolescence'.

As the idea was first tried at the very bottom of the late-1950s depression, it is perhaps not surprising that it lasted only until 1960 before being quietly abandoned; at least it saved the world from having to endure gruesome creations like the 1958 Oldsmobile for more than a year. The fairly clean lines of 1957 were dropped with the 1958 cars – the Dynamic 88, Super 88 and Ninety-Eight series, in a 16-model range. The 88s were built on the shorter of the year's two chassis lengths, on a 122.5-inch wheelbase. The two- and four-door hardtop Supers were in the upper series.

Without doubt, the main feature of the Super 88 was the way it looked. Beauty may be in the eye of the beholder but it would take a fair stretch of the imagination to describe the 1958 Olds as anything but ugly. Following the trend, it was huge, but shorn of its finery it was plain and square and, save for an obligatory dip in the doorline, it looked a little like a brick with a hardtop grafted on to it. Calling this 'the "Chrome King" of *all* cars' is a rare piece of understatement.

Massive fins, capped by chrome and with four horizontal chrome strips on their flanks, ran back to the gaudiest of tail-lights. The left-hand tail-light trim concealed the gas filler cap (it couldn't possibly have been for the sake of neatness), and dual back-up lamps were recessed into the bumper. The wildly over-decorated rear was 'balanced' at the front by a long horizontal moulding running around the dual headlights and back along to mid-car. The cheaper Dynamic just had a chrome strip around the moulding but the Super shunned restraint and filled it with a chrome panel. Maybe Olds just wanted to draw attention to the dual lights; it was the first time the division had used them. The Super 88s also had chrome spears along the rather elegant rooflines, and several more badges than the Dynamic.

It was a pity that the Super 88 looked so gross; mechanically it would have been a much happier car

had the 371cu in V8 not had so much superfluous sheet metal to carry around. The 371 had been introduced in the neat 1957 cars, replacing the earlier 324cu in V8. In 1958, power options ranged up to 312hp from engines equipped with the excellent J–2 Rocket set-up, using triple two-barrel carbs. The 1958 car actually wasn't much heavier than a year before, just bigger, so it would still run sub-10 seconds for 0–60mph, which was no embarrassment in most contemporary company; Oldsmobile hadn't completely lost track of its performance tradition.

Like several manufacturers around this period, Olds offered the option of air suspension. In the case of the 88 the option was known as New-Matic Ride and it meant a self-levelling system on all four wheels, plus double-acting shock absorbers all round. The suspension units

Model 1958 Oldsmobile
Super 88

Engine type ohv V8
Bore × stroke 4.0 × 3.688in
Capacity 371cu in
Compression ratio 10.0:1
Carburation 1 × 4bbl
Max. power 305hp
@ 4600rpm

Transmission Hydra-Matic

Wheelbase 122.5in
Weight 4008lb

Price $3112

Above: GM obviously hadn't
started worrying too much about
aerodynamics when they
designed the Super 88

Left: filler cap concealed in the tail
lamp housing – there was plenty
of room for it

Following pages: there was chrome
more or less everywhere on the
Super 88

were fed from an extra large, high-pressure air tank, and Old's air system was better than some, although it shared the reliability problems of most. Other options included a Trans-Portable transistor radio, which could be removed from the car and carried around as a portable.

In fairness to Oldsmobile, and to the 88s in particular, the division had not exactly cornered the market on appalling styling for 1958. Most of GM's marques gave best to the attractive Fords of the period (Edsel and Mercury notwithstanding) and Chrysler's new look left everyone else way behind anyway. It must, however, be some sort of reflection on the hypnotic effect that marketing had on the public that no one actually laughed out loud. In fact, in a year when overall industry output was at a disastrously low ebb, Oldsmobile did pretty well. They sold 310,795 cars during the calendar year. For the second time in the division's history, that meant fourth place in the industry sales league, Oldsmobile's best result.

The 1958 Oldsmobiles were none too wonderful one-year-wonders. The 1959 restyling brought slightly more subtle shapes with plenty of space and ample performance. Now, however, Oldsmobile was beginning to move away from such excesses as the 1958 and 1959 cars to join the compact revolution of the early 1960s. Most of the compacts were considerably more subtle than the 1958 Super 88s, but they may not be remembered for so long.

Buick Electra 225

THE END OF the decade heralded the end of glamour, 1950s style, and the beginning of glamour, 1960s style, a change from bulbous to sharp and from decorative to something nearer simplicity. It also very nearly heralded the end of Buick, whose recent history had been a list of one disaster after another. Little by little, from 1955 to 1959, Buick slipped from third to seventh in the market-place, but 1959 saw the beginning of an upturn in the division's fortunes.

Actually, 1959 sales were even worse than those of 1958, but at least Buick had started down a new road. Ed Ragsdale retired and a new general manager, Edward D. Rollert, was brought in to restore production quality and to rescue Buick's tarnished reputation. Harley Earl had taken an enormous amount of criticism over the 1957 and 1958 cars, particularly in view of Chrysler's new image, and for the 1959 cars he presented Ned Nickles with a clean sheet of paper and some firm outlines. Even the traditional Buick model names were laid to rest; in their places came Le Sabre, Invicta and Electra.

The Electra and the top-of-the-line Electra 225 series replaced the Supers and Roadmasters and they were totally different from the 1958 cars, which was no bad thing. Electra was taken from the Greek word for brilliant, and the 225 was so named because that was its overall length, a couple of inches short of the previous year's behemoth, the Limited. The new Buicks had been in preparation since mid-1956, and the 1959 model introduction was made very early, in September 1958.

The Electra 225, like the others, was naturally inspired by show cars such as the XP-300 and the Le Sabre, and its styling was really very clean and easy on the eye. It hinted strongly at aerodynamic efficiency, and its huge wedge-shaped rear fins canted outwards, in the Buick interpretation of the latest styling direction.

The Electra 225, which quickly gained the amusing nickname of 'Deuce and two bits', retained a version of the Fashion-Aire Dynastar Grille, now, thankfully, toned down and with far fewer chrome squares, above a simple, if heavy, front bumper. The front fender line swept up gracefully from the top edge of the grille, over angled dual headlights, and ran into a simple chrome strip along the car's sides, which, apart from the obligatory badges, was virtually the only superfluous decoration. Even the Buick trademarks, Sweepspear and Ventiports, were gone. With the windshield curving into the roofline, the Electras were some three to five inches lower than the 1958 cars and, in spite of a new chassis which allowed a lower floorpan and lower seats, they did lose a little headroom.

The new chassis, however, brought marked improvements in other directions. The Electra 225 used a 325hp version of the new, 401cu in V8, the Wildcat 445 (for 445lb ft of torque), and Twin Turbine Drive, the latest name for the Variable Pitch Dynaflow. Triple Turbine Drive and even a limited-slip differential were options. Power steering and power brakes were standard equipment and Buick's brakes were now probably the best in the industry. For 1959 the excellent aluminium-finned drums, which had recently appeared on the front, were fitted all round.

Better still, Buick were gradually accepting that the troublesome Air-Poise suspension was a real lemon and now it was offered on the rear only, with very few takers. The new K-frame, of semi-perimeter type with several cross-members, allowed the engine to be mounted further forward and the travel of the coil-spring suspension to be increased. The front and rear roll centres were changed and the handling was vastly improved, especially from the point of view of traction for the lusty engine. One minor mistake was the temporary abandonment of the front anti-sway bar which was hurriedly replaced for 1960. The latest power steering demanded less effort but gave more feel, and a degree of increase of effort with speed allowed much better stability. Furthermore, the steering was now much more reliable than of old.

There were seventeen Buick models for 1959 and only just over 232,000 cars were built, of which 5493 were Electra convertibles. Those figures show the extent of the sales resistance which Buick was then encountering, because the new cars were really quite good, especially in terms of value for money – the 225 convertible, for example, sold for a very reasonable $4192. Unfortunately, the marketing was not as good as the car and initial enthusiasm was allowed to evaporate during a break in production caused by a steel strike. By the time the lines started rolling again, customers had had time to think 'but this is a *Buick!*' and the recovery had to wait for another year and another restyling. Once again, curves were rounded out and edges softened, leaving the crisp 1959 Buicks behind, as another one-year-wonder to be appreciated much more in retrospect.

SPECIFICATION

Model 1959 Buick Electra
225 convertible

Engine type ohv V8
Bore × stroke 4.187 × 3.64in
Capacity 401cu in
Compression ratio 10.5:1
Carburation 1 × 4bbl
Max. power 325hp
@ 4400rpm

Transmission Twin Turbine

Wheelbase 126.3in
Weight 4562lb

Price $4192

Preceding pages, and below: after the bulbous shapes and excessive decorations of 1958's automobile crop, it was good to see a return to something a little simpler and more elegant in 1959. The Electra 225 set the scene for the change from round to sharp lines

Left: sanity and simplicity even returned to the dashboard on the 1959 Buick

ALL THROUGH THE 1950s the trend for overdoing the glamour had been growing, but 1959 was the year when the industry finally went completely overboard so far as styling was concerned. Since Cadillac, of all people, had started the trend when they sprouted tiny tail fins in the late 1940s (a million years ago by Detroit standards), American cars had used more and more outrageous shapes, bigger fins and grilles and more chrome, as a crutch on which to hobble from one expensive restyling to the next.

In the recession-hit year of 1958, the addition of more muscle and more metal (mostly plated, non-functional and cheap) had failed to reduce flagging sales, so for 1959 the Big Three went to even more exaggerated lengths; 1959's American autos were probably the biggest, flashiest and most tasteless of all time, and they said it all about the state of the art, and the nation, at that period. As ever, Chrysler's offerings were among the neatest, but to say, as many did, that Dodge's 1959 fins and finery were less extravagant than most is a bit like saying that Genghis Khan was more socially acceptable than Attila the Hun.

All 1959's cars were the American ad industry's idea of high style; on a brochure leaning heavily on the imagery of Ming vases and Old Masters, a mailman beams approvingly at the 1959 Dodge which obviously goes with them, class-wise. The catchline of the brochure is 'Reflects your Taste for Finer Things'. That was how they sold cars in 1959; if it said it in the ads, it had to be true. The truth was that the 1959 Dodge Custom Royal was based on the 1957 and 1958 Dodges, which in turn meant the Chrysler 'Swept Wing', Forward Look shape, updated by the simple expedient of piling on more trim. The same basic shell, on the same 122-inch wheelbase chassis, had been given side-by-side dual headlights with chromed eyebrows, for 1958; now it also gained a lighter front-end treatment, with a simpler anodized-aluminium grille and wrap-up bumpers. The heavy chrome overriders remained, but now they incorporated the front parking lights in what looked like huge chrome-plated toothpaste tube tops. The tail-end was more of the same, with four enormous tail-lights in chrome shells and great, pointed, two-tone and chrome fins.

Even two years after the AMA's attempt in 1957 to de-emphasize the horsepower race by 'recommending' an end to factory competition involvement, horsepower continued to climb. In 1958 the Red Ram V8 had been offered with the short-lived option of fuel injection; the bad news was the death of the hemi, replaced by the less efficient, but cheaper, wedge-head V8. The 1959 Custom Royal had options ranging up to 345hp from its 383cu in motor with twin-four-barrel D-500 kit – at almost $450 over the basic price. With all that chrome to

SPECIFICATION

Model 1959 Dodge Custom Royal

Engine type ohv V8
Bore × stroke 4.13 × 3.38in
Capacity 361cu in
Compression ratio 10.0:1
Carburation 1 × 4bbl
Max. power 305hp @ 4600rpm

Transmission Torque-Flite

Wheelbase 122in
Weight 3660lb

Price $3145

Preceding pages: it isn't always easy to remember that Dodge's fins were less exaggerated than most

Left: classic 1950s front end treatment, with toothpaste tube parking lights and plenty of glamour

Right: the mind boggles at the flair for interior design of the Dodge executive who ordered this green fur trim as original equipment when his new Dodge left the line

haul around this was a popular choice. The 1959 Dodge had a ladder chassis and ball-joint front suspension, with the option of 'Level Flite' Torsion Aire suspension, plus the largely ignored choice of air springs at the rear. The advertising boast was 'lets you corner without side sway, stop without brake dive'. For all the horsepower and handling claims, the average American driver wanted the easy life. To give an idea of prevailing priorities, over ninety-five per cent of buyers specified automatic transmission (push-button three-speed Torque Flite on the Custom Royal), two out of three wanted power steering, but only one in three went for power brakes.

The Custom Royal offered plenty of other attractions for its price range, such as an 'Indi-Color' speedometer which changed colours as speed was increased, electric windows, tinted glass and oversized tyres (for comfort, not speed), plus what was billed 'push-button weather', which was a neat trick if you could do it. The most novel item, though, was swivelling front seats, to make for easier entry and exit. These seats, in Jacquard fabric and vinyl, swung outwards through forty degrees, on nylon rollers, as the doors were opened, although the passenger still had to summon up enough energy from somewhere to climb out to the kerb without further assistance.

Such devices were clever, but they were really just short-lived gimmicks. They said a great deal about the direction auto development was taking as the 1950s lumbered to a close, with add-on eye-catchers pushing the role of basic engineering into the back seat. As these cars, with or without the gadgets, failed miserably to rekindle the necessary enthusiasm to part with dollar bills, the industry got set to change course again. The 1959 Custom Royal had definitely been the peak of Dodge's excursion into excess; from here on sanity would return. Sadly, the compacts which were already in the pipeline could not really count style among the list of benefits which they allegedly brought to the market; 1959 had been just too good a year to follow.

THERE WERE BIG changes at Pontiac in 1959, changes that had been coming since 1956, when Semon E. Knudsen took over the reins as Pontiac's General Manager. At forty-three years old, 'Bunkie' Knudsen became the youngest General Manager in any division of General Motors. He brought a much-needed new approach to Pontiac, which for many years had had the not altogether complimentary label of the most conservative division in GM. Under Bunkie's guidance, Pontiac would foster a fashionable 'youth image', based largely on performance cars. In the forefront of the new Pontiac style would be the Bonneville, first seen in 1957 as a limited-production convertible in the fast and flashy mould. In 1958 the 'Bold New Bonneville: Boldest Advance in 50 Years' was the Indy Pace Car and by 1959 Bonneville was the premier Pontiac series, alongside the low-priced Catalina and the mid-range Star Chief.

changed somewhat from the cars of the two previous years; as introduced in 1957, the convertible had been the fastest of all Pontiacs, with the option of three two-barrel carbs or fuel injection, and up to 310 horsepower. In this guise it sold less than 650 copies, but tricked up for 1958 and available as a hardtop as well as a convertible, it sold more than 12,000 cars, in spite of the recession.

Nevertheless, Bunkie liked a cleaner look. In 1935 his father, Bill, then General Manager at Pontiac, had introduced the famous 'Silver Streak' trademark of a broad, ribbed chrome appliqué running down the centre of all Pontiac hoods. It was one of the most recognizable of all corporate styling signatures; during the 1950s Pontiacs even grew two Silver Streaks. One of the first things that Bunkie did was to consign the Silver Streak to history, along with the famous Indian head

The first Bonnevilles had been fairly restrained in styling terms, but the 1958s had been totally overdone, with enormous sculpted side panels and the inevitable allusion to rocket power in the chrome side-spears. Fortunately for the future of good taste, 1958 was the first year of GM's new policy of 'planned obsolescence', whereby the market was to be treated to completely new cars every year, the theory being that nobody would want to be seen in *any* of 1958's appallingly gaudy offerings, and the industry had a generally very poor sales year.

The first chance Knudsen had had to offer something new from the ground up was in 1959, and the cars mercifully bore no resemblance whatsoever to the gross 1958s. The new Pontiacs were among the best looking of all 1959's offerings from GM, although Chrysler perhaps had the edge in styling. The 1959 Bonneville had

mascot behind which Pontiacs had stood for many a year. Pontiac had been a mid-eighteenth century Indian chief who banded together several tribes, primarily to resist British incursion. Being a local hero, he gave his name first to the town and eventually to the car that was built there. Chief Pontiac should have been a happy Indian, but his automobile effigy (in many incarnations) never smiled. In the fundamentally optimistic society of the 1950s, that may have been why he had to go.

The 1959 Pontiac Bonneville was stunningly different: it was long, low and extremely wide. Width was the main feature; the new Wide-Track engineering for the Pontiac range set the wheels a full five inches further apart than before, for the widest stance of any car of its day. It was also much more simply styled, with straighter lines, a new divided grille above a simple bumper, small twin-fins at the rear and a much neater

SPECIFICATION

Model 1959 Pontiac
  Bonneville

Engine type ohv V8
Bore × stroke 4.062 × 3.75in
Capacity 389cu in
Compression ratio 8.6:1
Carburation 1 × 4bbl
Max. power 260hp
  @ 4200rpm

Transmission Hydra-Matic

Wheelbase 124in
Weight 3487lb

Price $2867

Pages 140–41 and left: by 1959
Pontiac had dropped the famous
Silver Streak and even old Chief
Pontiac's grizzled countenance,
but plenty of new war paint was
put in their place as Pontiac set
out to pursue the 'youth market',
via looks and incredible
performance

Right: the last word on the 1950s
– if you've got it, flaunt it

use of the quad headlights introduced in 1958. The roof treatment varied across the Bonneville range, from the swept-back line of the two-door hardtop to the distinctive, flat-roofed 'Vista-Dome' of the four-door hardtop, which had an exaggerated-wraparound rear window. Knudsen's commitment to the sporting image was backed up by the ample power of the 1959 options, with up to 315hp available on the Bonneville from 389cu in, although the much bigger and heavier 1959 cars were not as quick or agile as the earlier Bonnevilles.

Wide-Track, combined with other engineering changes, allowed more space for better engine and brake cooling, and the lower centre of gravity and wide stance made this one of the smoothest-riding, best-handling cars of its day. With the exaggeratedly wide track sitting on a 124-inch wheelbase, the 1959 Pontiac actually looked the way that most other makes only looked in the artist's impressions in the ads and brochures. People liked the 1959 Bonneville and, between the two- and four-door hardtops and the convertible, the nameplate sold 82,500 models from a total Pontiac market of over 388,500, good enough to move the marque up from sixth to fifth place in the industry chart. Cars like the 1959 Bonneville were the swansong of the 1950s, and although the genre was to continue for some time yet, even Pontiac was already looking to combine the performance image with more conservative packaging; in 1960 the Tempest was introduced, in the vanguard of the compact invasion, with a four-cylinder engine derived from half the old Bonneville unit, and pointing the way out of a decade that could never be repeated.